For A Future To Be Possible

For A Future To Be Possible
Commentaries on the Five Mindfulness Trainings

Thich Nhat Hanh

with

Robert Aitken
Richard Baker
Stephen Batchelor
Patricia Marx Ellsberg
Joan Halifax
Chân Không
Maxine Hong Kingston
Jack Kornfield
Annabel Laity
Christopher Reed
Sulak Sivaraksa
Gary Snyder
David Steindl-Rast
Arthur Waskow

Parallax Press
Berkeley, California

Parallax Press
P.O. Box 7355
Berkeley, CA 94707

Design by Legacy Media
Cover photograph by Gaetano Kazuo Maida

Permission to use the following contributions is gratefully acknowledged: Jack
Kornfield's essay is excerpted from *Seeking the Heart of Wisdom*, by Joseph
Goldstein and Jack Kornfield. Copyright © 1987 by Joseph Goldstein and Jack
Kornfield. Reprinted by permission of Shambhala Publications. Gary Snyder's
essay was previously printed in *The Ten Directions*, journal of the Zen Center of
Los Angeles, Spring/Summer 1991, and is reprinted with permission of the au-
thor. Sulak Sivaraksa's essay is from *Seeds of Peace: A Buddhist Vision for Renewing
Society* (Berkeley: Parallax Press, 1991), and is reprinted with permission of the
publisher.

Library of Congress Cataloging-in-Publication Data
For a future to be possible : commentaries on the five mindfulness trainings /
Thich Nhat Hanh with Robert Aitken ... [et al.]. —Rev. ed.
    p. cm.
  ISBN 1-888375-07-8 (pbk.)
    1. Five Precepts (Buddhism) I. Nhât Hanh, Thích. II. Aitken, Rob-
ert. 1917—
BQ5495.F67 1998   97-36378
294.3'5—dc21   CIP

1 2 3 4 5 6 7 8 9 10 / 01 00 99 98 97

Contents

PART ONE

The Five Mindfulness Trainings

The Five Mindfulness Trainings

FIRST MINDFULNESS TRAINING

Aware of the suffering caused by the destruction of life, I am committed to cultivating compassion and learning ways to protect the lives of people, animals, plants, and minerals. I am determined not to kill, not to let others kill, and not to condone any act of killing in the world, in my thinking, and in my way of life.

SECOND MINDFULNESS TRAINING

Aware of the suffering caused by exploitation, social injustice, stealing, and oppression, I am committed to cultivating loving kindness and learning ways to work for the well-being of people, animals, plants, and minerals. I will practice generosity by sharing my time, energy, and material resources with those who are in real need. I am determined not to steal and not to possess anything that should belong to others. I will respect the property of others, but I will prevent others from profiting from human suffering or the suffering of other species on Earth.

THIRD MINDFULNESS TRAINING

Aware of the suffering caused by sexual misconduct, I am committed to cultivating responsibility and learning ways to protect the safety and integrity of individuals, couples, families, and society. I am determined not to engage in sexual relations without love and a long-term commitment. To preserve the happiness of myself and others, I am determined to respect my commitments and the commitments of others. I will do everything in my power to protect children from sexual abuse and to prevent couples and families from being broken by sexual misconduct.

FOURTH MINDFULNESS TRAINING

Aware of the suffering caused by unmindful speech and the inability to listen to others, I am committed to cultivating loving speech and deep listening in order to bring joy and happiness to others and relieve others of their suffering. Knowing that words can create happiness or suffering, I am determined to speak truthfully, with words that inspire self-confidence, joy, and hope. I will not spread news that I do not know to be certain and will not criticize or condemn things of which I am not sure. I will refrain from uttering words that can cause division or discord, or that can cause the family or the community to break. I am determined to make all efforts to reconcile and resolve all conflicts, however small.

FIFTH MINDFULNESS TRAINING

Aware of the suffering caused by unmindful consumption, I am committed to cultivating good health, both physical and mental, for myself, my family, and my society by practicing mindful eating, drinking, and consuming. I will ingest only items that preserve peace, well-being, and joy in my body, in my consciousness, and in the collective body and consciousness of my family and society. I am determined not to use alcohol or any other intoxicant or to ingest foods or other items that contain toxins, such as certain TV programs, magazines, books, films, and conversations. I am aware that to damage my body or my consciousness with these poisons is to betray my ancestors, my parents, my society, and future generations. I will work to transform violence, fear, anger, and confusion in myself and in society by practicing a diet for myself and for society. I understand that a proper diet is crucial for self-transformation and for the transformation of society.

Introduction

I have been in the West for thirty years, and for the past ten I have been leading mindfulness retreats in Europe, Australia, and North America. During these retreats, my students and I have heard many stories of suffering, and we have been dismayed to learn how much of this suffering is the result of alcoholism, drug abuse, sexual abuse, and similar behaviors that have been passed down from generation to generation.

There is a deep malaise in society. When we put a young person in this society without trying to protect him, he receives violence, hatred, fear, and insecurity every day, and eventually he gets sick. Our conversations, TV programs, advertisements, newspapers, and magazines all water the seeds of suffering in young people, and in not-so-young people as well. We feel a kind of vacuum in ourselves, and we try to fill it by eating, reading, talking, smoking, drinking, watching TV , going to the movies, or even overworking. Taking refuge in these things only makes us feel hungrier and less satisfied, and we want to ingest even more. We need some guidelines, some preventive medicine, to protect ourselves, so we can become healthy again. We have to find a cure for our illness. We have to find something that is good, beautiful, and true in which we can take refuge.

When we drive a car, we are expected to observe certain rules so that we do not have an accident. Two thousand five hundred years ago, the Buddha offered certain guidelines to his lay students to help them live peaceful, wholesome, and happy lives. They were the Five Mindfulness Trainings, and at the foundation of each of these mindfulness trainings is mindfulness. With mindfulness, we are aware of what is going on in our bodies, our feelings, our minds, and the world, and we avoid doing harm to ourselves and others. Mindfulness protects us, our families, and our society, and ensures a safe and happy present and a safe and happy future.

In Buddhism, mindfulness trainings, concentration, and insight always go together. It is impossible to speak of one without the other two. This is called the Threefold Train-ing—*śila*, the practice of the mindfulness trainings; *samadhi*, the practice of concentration; and *prajña*, the practice of insight. Mindfulness Trainings, concentration, and insight "inter-are." Practicing the mindfulness trainings brings about concentration, and concentration is needed for in-sight. Mindfulness is the ground for concentration, concen-tration allows us to look deeply, and insight is the fruit of looking deeply. When we are mindful, we can see that by refraining from doing "this," we prevent "that" from hap-pening. This kind of insight is not imposed on us by an outside authority. It is the fruit of our own observation. Practicing the mindfulness trainings, therefore, helps us be more calm and concentrated and brings more insight and enlightenment, which makes our practice of the mindfulness trainings more solid. The three are intertwined; each helps the other two, and all three bring us closer to final libera-tion—the end of "leaking." They prevent us from falling back into illusion and suffering. When we are able to step out of the stream of suffering, it is called *anasvara*, "to stop

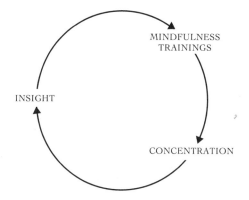

leaking." As long as we continue to leak, we are like a vessel with a crack, and inevitably we will fall into suffering, sorrow, and delusion.

The Five Mindfulness Trainings are love itself. To love is to understand, protect, and bring well-being to the object of our love. The practice of the trainings accomplishes this. We protect ourselves and we protect each other.

The translation of the Five Mindfulness Trainings presented in this book is new. It is the result of insights gained from practicing together as a community. A spiritual tradition is like a tree. It needs to be watered in order to bring forth new leaves and branches, so it can continue to be a living reality. We help the tree of Buddhism grow by living deeply the essence of reality, the practice of mindfulness trainings, concentration, and insight. If we continue to practice the mindfulness trainings deeply, in relation to our society and culture, I am confident that our children and their children will have an even better understanding of the Five Mindfulness Trainings and will obtain even deeper peace and joy.

Until recently, I have used the term "precepts" instead of "mindfulness trainings." But many Western friends told me that the word "precepts" evokes in them a strong feeling of good and evil, that if they "break" the precepts, they feel they have completely failed. Precepts are different from "commandments" and "rules." They are the insights born from mindful observation and direct experience of suffering. They are the guidelines that help us train ourselves to live in a way that protects us and those around us. As we continue the training, our understanding and practice of the precepts deepen. No one can be perfect when he or she just begins the training, and even during the time of training. Precepts are the most concrete expression of the practice of mindfulness. That is why it is appropriate and helpful to describe them as "mindfulness trainings."

In Buddhist circles, one of the first expressions of our desire to practice the way of understanding and love is to formally receive the Five Mindfulness Trainings from a teacher. During the ceremony, the teacher reads each training, and then the student repeats it and vows to study, practice, and observe the training read. It is remarkable to see the peace and happiness in someone the moment she receives the mindfulness trainings. Before making the decision to receive them, she may have felt confused, but with the decision to practice the mindfulness trainings, many bonds of attachment and confusion are cut. After the ceremony is over, you can see in her face that she has been liberated to a great extent.

When you vow to observe even one mindfulness training, that strong decision arising from your insight leads to real freedom and happiness. The community is there to support you and to witness the birth of your insight and determination. A mindfulness trainings ceremony has the power of cutting through, liberating, and building. After the ceremony, if you continue to practice the mindfulness trainings, looking deeply in order to have deeper insight concerning reality, your peace and liberation will increase. The way you practice the mindfulness trainings reveals the depth of your peace and the depth of your insight.

Whenever someone formally vows to study, practice, and observe the Five Mindfulness Trainings, he also takes refuge in the Three Jewels—*Buddha, Dharma,* and *Sangha.* Practicing the Five Mindfulness Trainings is a concrete expression of our appreciation and trust in these Three Jewels. The Buddha is mindfulness itself; the Dharma is the way of understanding and love; and the Sangha is the community that supports our practice.

The Five Mindfulness Trainings and the Three Jewels are worthy objects for our faith. They are not at all abstract—we can learn, practice, explore, extend, and check them against our own experience. To study and practice them will surely bring peace and happiness to ourselves, our community, and our society. We human beings need something to believe in, something that is good, beautiful, and true, something that we can touch. Faith in the practice of mindfulness—in the Five Mindfulness Trainings and the Three Jewels—is something anyone can discover, appreciate, and integrate into his or her daily life.

The Five Mindfulness Trainings and the Three Jewels have their equivalents in all spiritual traditions. They come from deep within us and practicing them helps us be more rooted in our own tradition. After you study the Five Mindfulness Trainings and the Three Jewels, I hope you will go back to your own tradition and shed light on the jewels that are already there. The Five Mindfulness Trainings are medicine for our time. I urge you to practice them the way they are presented here or as they are taught in your own tradition.

What is the best way to practice the mindfulness trainings? I do not know. I am still learning, along with you. I appreciate the phrase that is used in the Five Mindfulness Trainings: to "learn ways." We do not know everything. But we can minimize our ignorance. Confucius said, "To know that you don't know is the beginning of knowing." I think this is the way to practice. We should be modest and open so we can learn together. We need a Sangha, a community, to support us, and we need to stay in close touch with our society to practice the mindfulness trainings well. Many of today's problems did not exist at the time of the Buddha. Therefore, we have to look deeply together in order to develop the insights that will help us and our children find better ways to live wholesome, happy, and healthy lives.

When someone asks, "Do you care? Do you care about me? Do you care about life? Do you care about the Earth?", the best way to answer is to practice the Five Mindfulness Trainings. This is to teach with your actions and not just with words. If you really care, please practice these mindfulness trainings for your own protection and for the protection of other people and species. If we do our best to practice, a future will be possible for us, our children, and their children.

Reverence for Life

Aware of the suffering caused by the destruction of life, I am committed to cultivating compassion and learning ways to protect the lives of people, animals, plants, and minerals. I am determined not to kill, not to let others kill, and not to condone any act of killing in the world, in my thinking, and in my way of life.

Life is precious. It is everywhere, inside us and all around us; it has so many forms.

The First Mindfulness Training is born from the awareness that lives everywhere are being destroyed. We see the suffering caused by the destruction of life, and we vow to cultivate compassion and use it as a source of energy for the protection of people, animals, plants, and minerals. The First Mindfulness Training is a training of compassion, *karuna* — the ability to remove suffering and transform it. When we see suffering, compassion is born in us.

It is important for us to stay in touch with the suffering of the world. We need to nourish that awareness through many means — sounds, images, direct contact, visits, and so on — in order to keep compassion alive in us. But we must be careful not to take in too much. Any remedy must be taken in the proper dosage. We need to stay in touch with suffering only to the extent that we will not forget, so that compassion will flow within us and be a source of energy for our actions. If we use anger at injustice as the source for our energy, we may do something harmful, something that we will later regret. According to Buddhism, compassion is the only source of energy that is useful and safe. With compassion, your energy is born from insight; it is not blind energy.

We humans are made entirely of nonhuman elements, such as plants, minerals, earth, clouds, and sunshine. For our practice to be deep and true, we must include the eco-system. If the environment is destroyed, humans will be de-stroyed, too. Protecting human life is not possible without also protecting the lives of animals, plants, and minerals. The *Diamond Sutra* teaches us that it is impossible to distin-guish between sentient and non-sentient beings. This is one of many ancient Buddhist texts that teach deep ecology. Every Buddhist practitioner should be a protector of the en-vironment. Minerals have their own lives, too. In Buddhist monasteries, we chant, "Both sentient and non-sentient beings will realize full enlightenment." The First Mindful-ness Training is the practice of protecting all lives, includ-ing the lives of minerals.

"I am determined not to kill, not to let others kill, and not to condone any act of killing in the world, in my thinking, and in my way of life." We cannot support any act of killing; no killing can be justified. But not to kill is not enough. We must also learn ways to prevent others from killing. We cannot say, "I am not responsible. They did it. My hands are clean." If you were in Germany during the time of the Nazis, you could not say, "They did it. I did not." If, during the Gulf War, you did not say or do anything to try to stop the kill-ing, you were not practicing this training. Even if what you

said or did failed to stop the war, what is important is that you tried, using your insight and compassion.

It is not just by not killing with your body that you observe the First Mindfulness Training. If in your thinking you allow the killing to go on, you also break this training. We must be determined not to condone killing, even in our minds. According to the Buddha, the mind is the base of all actions. It is most dangerous to kill in the mind. When you believe, for example, that yours is the only way for humankind and that everyone who follows another way is your enemy, millions of people could be killed because of that idea.

Thinking is at the base of everything. It is important for us to put an eye of awareness into each of our thoughts. Without a correct understanding of a situation or a person, our thoughts can be misleading and create confusion, despair, anger, or hatred. Our most important task is to develop correct insight. If we see deeply into the nature of interbeing, that all things "inter-are," we will stop blaming, arguing, and killing, and we will become friends with everyone. To practice nonviolence, we must first of all learn ways to deal peacefully with ourselves. If we create true harmony within ourselves, we will know how to deal with family, friends, and associates.

When we protest against a war, for example, we may assume that we are a peaceful person, a representative of peace, but this might not be true. If we look deeply, we will observe that the roots of war are in the unmindful ways we have been living. We have not sown enough seeds of peace and understanding in ourselves and others, therefore we are co-responsible: "Because I have been like this, they are like that." A more holistic approach is the way of "interbeing": "This is like this, because that is like that." This is the way of understanding and love. With this insight, we can see clearly and help our government see clearly. Then we can go to a demonstration and say, "This war is unjust, destructive, and not worthy of our great nation." This is far more effective than angrily condemning others. Anger always accelerates the damage.

All of us, even pacifists, have pain inside. We feel angry and frustrated, and we need to find someone willing to listen to us who is capable of understanding our suffering. In Buddhist iconography, there is a bodhisattva named Avalokitesvara who has one thousand arms and one thousand hands, and has an eye in the palm of each hand. One thousand hands represent action, and the eye in each hand represents understanding. When you understand a situation or a person, any action you do will help and will not cause more suffering. When you have an eye in your hand, you will know how to practice true nonviolence.

To practice nonviolence, first of all we have to practice it within ourselves. In each of us, there is a certain amount of violence and a certain amount of nonviolence. Depending on our state of being, our response to things will be more or less nonviolent. Even if we take pride in being vegetarian, for example, we have to acknowledge that the water in which we boil our vegetables contains many tiny microorganisms. We cannot be completely nonviolent, but by being vegetarian, we are going in the direction of nonviolence. If we want to head north, we can use the North Star to guide us, but it is impossible to arrive at the North Star. Our effort is only to proceed in that direction.

Anyone can practice some nonviolence, even army generals. They may, for example, conduct their operations in ways that avoid killing innocent people. To help soldiers move in a nonviolent direction, we have to be in touch with them. If we divide reality into two camps—the violent and the nonviolent—and stand in one camp while attacking the other, the world will never have peace. We will always blame and condemn those we feel are responsible for wars and social injustice, without recognizing the degree of violence in ourselves. We must work on ourselves and also work with those we condemn if we want to have a real impact.

It never helps to draw a line and dismiss some people as enemies, even those who act violently. We have to approach them with love in our hearts and do our best to help them move in a direction of nonviolence. If we work for peace out of anger, we will never succeed. Peace is not an end. It can never come about through non-peaceful means.

Most important is to *become* nonviolence, so that when a situation presents itself, we will not create more suffering. To practice nonviolence, we need gentleness, loving kindness, compassion, joy, and equanimity directed to our bodies, our feelings, and other people. With mindfulness—the practice of peace—we can begin by working to transform the wars in ourselves. There are techniques for doing this. Conscious breathing is one. Every time we feel upset, we can stop what we are doing, refrain from saying anything, and breathe in and out several times, aware of each in-breath and each out-breath. If we are still upset, we can go for walking meditation, mindful of each slow step and each breath we take. By cultivating peace within, we bring about peace in society. It depends on us. To practice peace in ourselves is to minimize the numbers of wars between this and that feeling, or this and that perception, and we can then have real peace with others as well, including the members of our own family.

I am often asked, "What if you are practicing nonviolence and someone breaks into your house and tries to kidnap your daughter or kill your husband? What should you do? Should you still act in a nonviolent way?" The answer depends on your state of being. If you are prepared, you may react calmly and intelligently, in the most nonviolent way possible. But to be ready to react with intelligence and nonviolence, you have to train yourself in advance. It may take ten years, or longer. If you wait until the time of crisis to ask the question, it will be too late. A this-or-that kind of answer would be superficial. At that crucial moment, even if you know that nonviolence is better than violence, if your understanding is only intellectual and not in your whole being, you will not act nonviolently. The fear and anger in you will prevent you from acting in the most nonviolent way.

We have to look deeply every day to practice this training well. Every time we buy or consume something, we may be condoning some form of killing.

While practicing the protection of humans, animals, plants, and minerals, we know that we are protecting ourselves. We feel in permanent and loving touch with all species on Earth. We are protected by the mindfulness and loving kindness of the Buddha and many generations of Sanghas who also practice this mindfulness training. This energy of loving kindness brings us the feeling of safety, health, and joy, and this becomes real the moment we make the decision to receive and practice the First Mindfulness Training.

Feeling compassion is not enough. We have to learn to express it. That is why love must go together with understanding. Understanding and insight show us how to act.

Our real enemy is forgetfulness. If we nourish mindfulness every day and water the seeds of peace in ourselves and those around us, we become alive, and we can help ourselves and others realize peace and compassion.

Life is so precious, yet in our daily lives we are usually carried away by our forgetfulness, anger, and worries, lost in the past, unable to touch life in the present moment. When we are truly alive, everything we do or touch is a miracle. To practice mindfulness is to return to life in the present moment. The practice of the First Mindfulness Training is a celebration of reverence for life. When we appreciate and honor the beauty of life, we will do everything in our power to protect all life.

Generosity

Aware of the suffering caused by exploitation, social injustice, stealing, and oppression, I am committed to cultivating loving kindness and learning ways to work for the well-being of people, animals, plants, and minerals. I will practice generosity by sharing my time, energy, and material resources with those who are in real need. I am determined not to steal and not to possess anything that should belong to others. I will respect the property of others, but I will prevent others from profiting from human suffering or the suffering of other species on Earth.

Exploitation, social injustice, and stealing come in many forms. Oppression is one form of stealing that causes much suffering both here and in the Third World. The moment we vow to cultivate loving kindness, loving kindness is born in us, and we make every effort to stop exploitation, social injustice, stealing, and oppression.

In the First Mindfulness Training, we found the word "compassion." Here, we find the words "loving kindness." Compassion and loving kindness are the two aspects of love taught by the Buddha. Compassion, karuna in Sanskrit and Pali, is the intention and capacity to relieve the suffering of another person or living being. Loving kindness, *maitri* in Sanskrit, *metta* in Pali, is the intention and capacity to bring joy and happiness to another person or living being. It was predicted by Shakyamuni Buddha that the next Buddha will bear the name Maitreya, the Buddha of Love.

"Aware of the suffering caused by exploitation, social injustice, stealing, and oppression, I am committed to cultivating loving kindness and learning ways to work for the well-being of people, animals, plants, and minerals." Even with maitri as a source of energy in ourselves, we still need to learn to look deeply in order to find ways to express it. We do it as individuals, and we learn ways to do it as a nation. To promote the well-being of people, animals, plants, and minerals, we have to come together as a community and examine our situation, exercising our intelligence and our ability to look deeply so that we can discover appropriate ways to express our maitri in the midst of real problems.

Suppose you want to help those who are suffering under a dictatorship. In the past you may have tried sending in troops to overthrow their government, but you have learned that when doing that, you cause the deaths of many innocent people, and even then, you might not overthrow the dictator. If you practice looking more deeply, with loving kindness, to find a better way to help these people without causing suffering, you may realize that the best time to help is before the country falls into the hands of a dictator. If you offer the young people of that country the opportunity to learn your democratic ways of governing by giving them scholarships to come to your country, that would be a good investment for peace in the future. If you had done that thirty years ago, the other country might be democratic now, and you would not have to bomb them or send in troops to "liberate" them. This is just one example of how looking deeply and learning can help us find ways to do things that are more in line with loving kindness. If we wait until the situation gets bad, it may be too late. If we practice the mindfulness trainings together with politicians, soldiers, businesspeople, lawyers, legislators, artists, writers, and teachers, we can find the best ways to practice compassion, loving kindness, and understanding.

It requires time to practice generosity. We may want to help those who are hungry, but we are caught in the problems of our own daily lives. Sometimes, one pill or a little rice could save the life of a child, but we do not take the time to help, because we think we do not have the time. In Ho Chi Minh City, for example, there are street children who call themselves "the dust of life." They are homeless, and they wander the streets by day and sleep under trees at night. They scavenge in garbage heaps to find things like plastic bags they can sell for one or two cents per pound. The nuns and monks in Ho Chi Minh City have opened their temples to these children, and if the children agree to stay four hours in the morning—learning to read and write and playing with the monks and nuns—they are offered a vegetarian lunch. Then they can go to the Buddha hall for a nap. (In Vietnam, we always take naps after lunch; it is so hot. When the Americans came, they brought their practice of working eight hours, from nine to five. Many of us tried, but we could not do it. We desperately need our naps after lunch.)

Then, at two o'clock, there is more teaching and playing with the children, and children who stay for the afternoon receive dinner. The temple does not have a place for them to sleep overnight. In our community in France, we have been supporting these nuns and monks. It costs only twenty cents for a child to have both lunch and dinner, and it will keep him from being out on the streets, where he might steal cigarettes, smoke, use delinquent language, and learn the worst behavior. By encouraging the children to go to the temple, we help prevent them from becoming delinquent and entering prison later on. It takes time to help these children, not much money. There are so many simple things like this we can do to help people, but because we cannot free ourselves from our situation and our lifestyle, we do nothing at all. We need to come together as a community, and, looking deeply, find ways to free ourselves so we can practice the Second Mindfulness Training.

"I will practice generosity by sharing my time, energy, and material resources with those who are in real need." This sentence is clear. The feeling of generosity and the capacity for being generous are not enough. We also need to express our generosity. We may feel that we don't have the time to make people happy—we say, "Time is money," but time is more than money. Life is for more than using time to make money. Time is for being alive, for sharing joy and happiness with others. The wealthy are often the least able to make others happy. Only those with time can do so.

I know a man named Bac Siêu in Thua Thiên Province in Vietnam, who has been practicing generosity for fifty years; he is a living bodhisattva. With only a bicycle, he visits villages of thirteen provinces, bringing something for this family and something for that family. When I met him in 1965, I was a little too proud of our School of Youth for Social Service. We had begun to train three hundred workers, including monks and nuns, to go out to rural villages

to help people rebuild homes and modernize local economies, health-care systems, and education. Eventually we
had ten thousand workers throughout the country. As I was
telling Bac Siêu about our projects, I was looking at his
bicycle and thinking that with a bicycle he could help only
a few people. But when the communists took over and
closed our School, Bac Siêu continued, because his way of
working was formless. Our orphanages, dispensaries,
schools, and resettlement centers were all shut down or
taken by the government. Thousands of our workers had
to stop their work and hide. But Bac Siêu had nothing to
take. He was truly a bodhisattva, working for the well-being
of others. I feel more humble now concerning the ways of
practicing generosity.

The war created many thousands of orphans. Instead of
raising money to build orphanages, we sought people in the
West to sponsor a child. We found families in the villages
to each take care of one orphan, then we sent $6 every
month to that family to feed the child and send him or her
to school. Whenever possible, we tried to place the child in
the family of an aunt, an uncle, or a grandparent. With just
$6, the child was fed and sent to school, and the rest of the
children in the family were also helped. Children benefit
from growing up in a family. Being in an orphanage can be
like being in the army—children do not grow up naturally.
If we look for and learn ways to practice generosity, we will
improve all the time.

*"I am determined not to steal and not to possess anything that
should belong to others. I will respect the property of others, but
I will prevent others from profiting from human suffering or the*

suffering of other species on Earth." When you practice one mindfulness training deeply, you will discover that you are practicing all five. The First Mindfulness Training is about taking life, which is a form of stealing—stealing the most precious thing someone has, his or her life. When we meditate on the Second Mindfulness Training, we see that stealing, in the forms of exploitation, social injustice, and oppression, are acts of killing—killing slowly by exploitation, by maintaining social injustice, and by political and economic oppression. Therefore, the Second Mindfulness Training has much to do with the mindfulness training of not killing. We see the "interbeing" nature of the first two mindfulness trainings. This is true of all Five Mindfulness Trainings. Some people formally receive just one or two mindfulness trainings. I didn't mind, because if you practice one or two mindfulness trainings deeply, all Five Mindfulness Trainings will be observed.

The Second Mindfulness Training is not to steal. Instead of stealing, exploiting, or oppressing, we practice generosity. In Buddhism, we say there are three kinds of gifts. The first is the gift of material resources. The second is to help people rely on themselves, to offer them the technology and know-how to stand on their own feet. Helping people with the Dharma so they can transform their fear, anger, and depression belongs to the second kind of gift. The third is the gift of non-fear. We are afraid of many things. We feel insecure, afraid of being alone, afraid of sickness and dying. To help people not be destroyed by their fears, we practice the third kind of gift-giving.

The Bodhisattva Avalokitesvara is someone who practices this extremely well. In the *Heart Sutra,* he teaches us the way to transform and transcend fear and ride on the waves of birth and death, smiling. He says that there is no production, no destruction, no being, no nonbeing, no increasing, and no decreasing. Hearing this helps us look deeply into the nature of reality to see that birth and death, being and nonbeing, coming and going, increasing and decreasing are all just ideas that we ascribe to reality, while reality transcends all concepts. When we realize the inter-being nature of all things—that even birth and death are just concepts—we transcend fear.

In 1991, I visited a friend in New York who was dying, Alfred Hassler. We had worked together in the peace movement for almost thirty years. Alfred looked as though he had been waiting for me to come before dying, and he died only a few hours after our visit. I went with my closest colleague, Sister Chân Không (True Emptiness).

Alfred was not awake when we arrived. His daughter Laura tried to wake him up, but she couldn't. So I asked Sister Chân Không to sing Alfred the *Song of No Coming and No Going:* "These eyes are not me, I am not caught by these eyes. This body is not me, I am not caught by this body. I am life without boundaries. I have never been born, I will never die." The idea is taken from the *Samyutta Nikaya.* She sang so beautifully, and I saw streams of tears running down the faces of Alfred's wife and children. They were tears of understanding, and they were very healing.

Suddenly, Alfred came back to himself. Sister Chân Không began to practice what she had learned from studying the sutra *The Teaching Given to the Sick*. She said, "Alfred, do you remember the times we worked together?" She evoked many happy memories we had shared together, and Alfred was able to remember each of them. Although he was obviously in pain, he smiled. This practice brought results right away. When a person is suffering from so much physical pain, we sometimes can alleviate his suffering by watering the seeds of happiness that are in him. A kind of balance is restored, and he will feel less pain.

All the while, I was practicing massage on his feet, and I asked him whether he felt my hand on his body. When you are dying, areas of your body become numb, and you feel as if you have lost those parts of your body. Doing massage in mindfulness, gently, gives the dying person the feeling that he is alive and being cared for. He knows that love is there. Alfred nodded, and his eyes seemed to say, "Yes, I feel your hands. I know my foot is there."

Sister Chân Không asked, "Do you know we learned a lot from you when we lived and worked together? The work you began, many of us are continuing to do. Please don't worry about anything." She told him many things like that, and he seemed to suffer less. At one point, he opened his mouth and said, "Wonderful, wonderful." Then, he sank back to sleep.

Before we left, we encouraged the family to continue these practices. The next day I learned that Alfred passed away just five hours after our visit. This was a kind of gift that belongs to the third category. If you can help people feel safe, less afraid of life, people, and death, you are practicing the third kind of gift.

During my meditation, I had a wonderful image—the shape of a wave, its beginning and its end. When conditions are sufficient, we perceive the wave, and when conditions are no longer sufficient, we do not perceive the wave. Waves are only made of water. We cannot label the wave as existing or nonexisting. After what we call the death of the wave, nothing is gone, nothing is lost. The wave has been absorbed into other waves, and somehow, time will bring the wave back again. There is no increasing, decreasing, birth, or death. When we are dying, if we think that everyone else is alive and we are the only person dying, our feeling of loneliness may be unbearable. But if we are able to visualize hundreds of thousands of people dying with us, our dying may become serene and even joyful. "I am dying in community. Millions of living beings are also dying in this very moment. I see myself together with millions of other living beings; we die in the Sangha. At the same time, millions of beings are coming to life. All of us are doing this together. I have been born, I am dying. We participate in the whole event as a Sangha." That is what I saw in my meditation. In the *Heart Sutra,* Avalokitesvara shares this kind of insight and helps us transcend fear, sorrow, and pain. The gift of non-fear brings about a transformation in us.

The Second Mindfulness Training is a deep practice. We speak of time, energy, and material resources, but time is not only for energy and material resources. Time is for being with others—being with a dying person or with someone who is suffering. Being really present for even five minutes can be a very important gift. Time is not just to make money. It is to produce the gift of Dharma and the gift of non-fear.

Sexual Responsibility

Aware of the suffering caused by sexual misconduct, I am committed to cultivating responsibility and learning ways to protect the safety and integrity of individuals, couples, families, and society. I am determined not to engage in sexual relations without love and a long-term commitment. To preserve the happiness of myself and others, I am determined to respect my commitments and the commitments of others. I will do everything in my power to protect children from sexual abuse and to prevent couples and families from being broken by sexual misconduct.

So many individuals, children, couples, and families have been destroyed by sexual misconduct. To practice the Third Mindfulness Training is to heal ourselves and heal our society. This is mindful living.

The Fifth Mindfulness Training—not to consume alcohol, toxins, or drugs—and the Third Mindfulness Training are linked. Both concern destructive and destabilizing behavior. These trainings are the right medicine to heal us. We need only to observe ourselves and those around us to see the truth. Our stability and the stability of our families and society cannot be obtained without the practice of these two trainings. If you look at individuals and families who are unstable and unhappy, you will see that many of them do not practice these trainings. You can make the diagnosis by yourself and then know that the medicine is there. Practicing these trainings is the best way to restore stability in the family and in society. For many people, this mindfulness training is easy to practice, but for others, it is quite difficult. It is important for these people to come together and share their experiences.

In the Buddhist tradition, we speak of the oneness of body and mind. Whatever happens to the body also happens to the mind. The sanity of the body is the sanity of the mind; the violation of the body is the violation of the mind. When we are angry, we may think that we are angry in our feelings, not in our body, but that is not true. When we love someone, we want to be close to him or her physically, but when we are angry at someone, we don't want to touch or be touched by that person. We cannot say that body and mind are separate.

A sexual relationship is an act of communion between body and spirit. This is a very important encounter, not to be done in a casual manner. You know that in your soul there are certain areas — memories, pain, secrets — that are private, that you would only share with the person you love and trust the most. You do not open your heart and show it to just anyone. In the imperial city, there is a zone you cannot approach called the forbidden city; only the king and his family are permitted to circulate there. There is a place like that in your soul that you do not allow anyone to approach except the one you trust and love the most.

The same is true of our body. Our bodies have areas that we do not want anyone to touch or approach unless he or she is the one we respect, trust, and love the most. When we are approached casually or carelessly, with an attitude that is less than tender, we feel insulted in our body and soul. Someone who approaches us with respect, tenderness, and utmost care is offering us deep communication, deep communion. It is only in that case that we will not feel hurt, misused, or abused, even a little. This cannot be attained unless there is true love and commitment. Casual sex cannot be described as love. Love is deep, beautiful, and whole.

True love contains respect. In my tradition, husband and wife are expected to respect each other like guests, and when you practice this kind of respect, your love and happiness will continue for a long time. In sexual relationships, respect is one of the most important elements. Sexual communion should be like a rite, a ritual performed in mindfulness with great respect, care, and love. If you are motivated by some desire, that is not love. Desire is not love. Love is something much more responsible. It has care in it.

We have to restore the meaning of the word "love." We have been using it in a careless way. When we say, "I love hamburgers," we are not talking about love. We are talking about our appetite, our desire for hamburgers. We should not dramatize our speech and misuse words like that. We make words like "love" sick that way. We have to make an effort to heal our language by using words carefully. The word "love" is a beautiful word. We have to restore its meaning.

"I am determined not to engage in sexual relations without love and a long-term commitment." If the word "love" is understood in the deepest way, why do we need to say "long-term commitment"? If love is real, we do not need long or short-term commitments, or even a wedding ceremony. True love

includes the sense of responsibility, accepting the other person as he is, with all his strengths and weaknesses. If we like only the best things in the person, that is not love. We have to accept his weaknesses and bring our patience, understanding, and energy to help him transform. Love is maitri, the capacity to bring joy and happiness, and karuna, the capacity to transform pain and suffering. This kind of love can only be good for people. It cannot be described as negative or destructive. It is safe. It guarantees everything.

Should we cross out the phrase "long-term commitment" or change it to "short-term commitment"? "Short-term commitment" means that we can be together for a few days and after that the relationship will end. That cannot be described as love. If we have that kind of relationship with another person, we cannot say that the relationship comes out of love and care. The expression "long-term commitment" helps people understand the word love. In the context of real love, commitment can only be long-term. "I want to love you. I want to help you. I want to care for you. I want you to be happy. I want to work for happiness. But just for a few days." Does this make sense?

You are afraid to make a commitment—to the trainings, to your partner, to anything. You want freedom. But remember, you have to make a long-term commitment to love your son deeply and help him through the journey of life as long as you are alive. You cannot just say, "I don't love you anymore." When you have a good friend, you also make a long-term commitment. You need her. How much more so with someone who wants to share your life, your soul, and your body. The phrase "long-term commitment" cannot express the depth of love, but we have to say something so that people understand.

A long-term commitment between two people is only a beginning. We also need the support of friends and other people. That is why, in our society, we have a wedding ceremony. The two families join together with other friends to witness the fact that you have come together to live as a couple. The priest and the marriage license are just symbols. What is important is that your commitment is witnessed by many friends and both of your families. Now you will be supported by them. A long-term commitment is stronger and more long-lasting if made in the context of a Sangha.

Your strong feelings for each other are very important, but they are not enough to sustain your happiness. Without other elements, what you describe as love may turn into something sour rather soon. The support of friends and family coming together weaves a kind of web. The strength of your feelings is only one of the strands of that web. Supported by many elements, the couple will be solid, like a tree. If a tree wants to be strong, it needs a number of roots sent deep into the soil. If a tree has only one root, it may be blown over by the wind. The life of a couple also needs to be supported by many elements—families, friends, ideals, practice, and Sangha.

In Plum Village, the practice community where I live in France, every time we have a wedding ceremony, we invite the whole community to celebrate and bring support to the couple. After the ceremony, on every full moon day, the couple recites the Five Awarenesses together, remembering that friends everywhere are supporting their relationship to be stable, long-lasting, and happy.* Whether or not your relationship is bound by law, it will be stronger and more long-lasting if made in the presence of a Sangha—friends who love you and want to support you in the spirit of understanding and loving kindness.

Love can be a kind of sickness. In the West and in Asia, we have the word "lovesick." What makes us sick is attachment. Although it is a sweet internal formation, this kind of love with attachment is like a drug. It makes us feel wonderful, but once we are addicted, we cannot have peace. We cannot study, do our daily work, or sleep. We only think of the object of our love. We are sick with love. This kind of love is linked to our willingness to possess and monopolize. We want the object of our love to be entirely ours and only for us. It is totalitarian. We do not want anyone to prevent us from being with him or her. This kind of love can be described as a prison, where we lock up our beloved and create only suffering for him or her. The one who is loved is deprived of freedom—of the right to be him or herself and enjoy life. This kind of love cannot be described as maitri or karuna. It is only the willingness to make use of the other person in order to satisfy our own needs.

When you have sexual energy that makes you feel unhappy, as though you are losing your inner peace, you

---

* The Five Awarenesses are: 1. We are aware that all generations of our ancestors and all future generations are present in us. 2. We are aware of the expectations that our ancestors, our children, and their children have of us. 3. We are aware that our joy, peace, freedom, and harmony are the joy, peace, freedom, and harmony of our ancestors, our children, and their children. 4. We are aware that understanding is the very foundation of love. 5. We are aware that blaming and arguing never help us and only create a wider gap between us, that only understanding, trust, and love can help us change and grow.

should know how to practice so that you do not do things that will bring suffering to other people or yourself. We have to learn about this. In Asia, we say there are three sources of energy—sexual, breath, and spirit. *Tinh*, sexual energy, is the first. When you have more sexual energy than you need, there will be an imbalance in your body and in your being. You need to know how to reestablish the balance, or you may act irresponsibly. According to Taoism and Buddhism, there are practices to help reestablish that balance, such as meditation or martial arts. You can learn the ways to channel your sexual energy into deep realizations in the domains of art and meditation.

The second source of energy is *khi*, breath energy. Life can be described as a process of burning. In order to burn, every cell in our body needs nutrition and oxygen. In his *Fire Sermon*, the Buddha said, "The eyes are burning, the nose is burning, the body is burning." In our daily lives, we have to cultivate our energy by practicing proper breathing. We benefit from the air and its oxygen, so we have to be sure that nonpolluted air is available to us. Some people cultivate their khi by refraining from smoking and talking, or by practicing conscious breathing after talking a lot. When you speak, take the time to breathe. At Plum Village, every time we hear the bell of mindfulness, everyone stops what they are doing and breathes consciously three times. We practice this way to cultivate and preserve our khi energy.

The third source of energy is *thân*, spirit energy. When you don't sleep at night, you lose some of this kind of energy. Your nervous system becomes exhausted and you cannot study or practice meditation well, or make good decisions. You don't have a clear mind because of lack of sleep or from worrying too much. Worry and anxiety drain this source of energy.

So don't worry. Don't stay up too late. Keep your nervous system healthy. Prevent anxiety. These kinds of practices cultivate the third source of energy. You need this source of energy to practice meditation well. A spiritual breakthrough requires the power of your spirit energy, which comes about through concentration and knowing how to preserve this source of energy. When you have strong spirit energy, you only have to focus it on an object, and you will have a breakthrough. If you don't have thân, the light of your concentration will not shine brightly, because the light emitted is very weak.

According to Asian medicine, the power of thân is linked to the power of tinh. When we expend our sexual energy, it takes time to restore it. In Chinese medicine, when you want to have a strong spirit and concentration, you are advised to refrain from having sexual relationships or overeating. You will be given herbs, roots, and medicine to enrich your source of thân, and, during the time you are taking this medicine, you are asked to refrain from sexual relationships. If your source of spirit is weak and you continue to have sexual relations, it is said that you cannot recover your spirit energy. Those who practice meditation should try to preserve their sexual energy, because they need it during meditation. If you are an artist, you may wish to practice channeling your sexual energy together with your spirit energy into your art.

During his struggle against the British, Gandhi under-
took many hunger strikes, and he recommended to his
friends who joined him on these fasts not to have sexual intercourse. When you fast for many days, if you have sexual
relations, you may die; you have to preserve your energies.
Thich Tri Quang, my friend who fasted for one hundred
days in the hospital in Saigon in 1966, knew very well that
not having sexual intercourse was very basic. Of course, as
a monk, he did not have any problem with that. He also
knew that speaking is an energy drain, so he refrained from
speaking. If he needed something, he said it in one or two
words or wrote it down. Writing, speaking, or making too
many movements draws from these three sources of energy.
So, the best thing is to lie down on your back and practice
deep breathing. This brings into you the vitality that you
need to survive a hundred-day hunger strike. If you don't
eat, you cannot replenish this energy. If you refrain from
studying, doing research, or worrying, you can preserve
these resources. These three sources of energy are linked
to each other. By practicing one, you help the other. That
is why *anapanasati,* the practice of conscious breathing, is
so important for our spiritual life. It helps with all of our
sources of energy.

Monks and nuns do not engage in sexual relationships
because they want to devote their energy to having a breakthrough in meditation. They learn to channel their sexual
energy to strengthen their spirit energy for the breakthrough. They also practice deep breathing to increase the
spirit energy. Since they live alone, without a family, they
can devote most of their time to meditation and teaching,

helping the people who provide them with food, shelter, and so on. They have contact with the population in the village in order to share the Dharma. Since they do not have a house or a family to care for, they have the time and space to do the things they like the most—walking, sitting, breathing, and helping fellow monks, nuns, and laypeople—and to realize what they want. Monks and nuns don't marry in order to preserve their time and energy for the practice.

"Responsibility" is the key word in the Third Mindfulness Training. In a community of practice, if there is no sexual misconduct, if the community practices this mindfulness training well, there will be stability and peace. This mindfulness training should be practiced by everyone. You respect, support, and protect each other as Dharma brothers and sisters. If you don't practice this mindfulness training, you may become irresponsible and create trouble in the community and in the community at large. We have all seen this. If a teacher cannot refrain from sleeping with one of his or her students, he or she will destroy everything, possibly for several generations. We need mindfulness in order to have that sense of responsibility. We refrain from sexual misconduct because we are responsible for the well-being of so many people. If we are irresponsible, we can destroy everything. By practicing this mindfulness training, we keep the Sangha beautiful.

In sexual relationships, people can get wounded. Practicing this mindfulness training is to prevent ourselves and others from being wounded. Often we think it is the woman who receives the wound, but men also get deeply wounded. We have to be very careful, especially in short-term commitments. The practice of the Third Mindfulness Training is a very strong way of restoring stability and peace in ourselves, our family, and our society. We should take the time to discuss problems relating to the practice of this mindfulness training, like loneliness, advertising, and even the sex industry.

The feeling of loneliness is universal in our society. There is no communication between ourselves and other people, even in the family, and our feeling of loneliness pushes us into having sexual relationships. We believe in a naive way that having a sexual relationship will make us feel less lonely, but it isn't true. When there is not enough communication with another person on the level of the heart and spirit, a sexual relationship will only widen the gap and destroy us both. Our relationship will be stormy, and we will make each other suffer. The belief that having a sexual relationship will help us feel less lonely is a kind of superstition. We should not be fooled by it. In fact, we will feel more lonely afterwards.

The union of the two bodies can only be positive when there is understanding and communion on the level of the heart and the spirit. Even between husband and wife, if the communion on the level of heart and spirit does not exist, the coming together of the two bodies will only separate you further. When that is the case, I recommend that you refrain from having sexual relationships and first try to make a breakthrough in communication.

There are two Vietnamese words, *tinh* and *nghĩa*, that are difficult to translate into English. They both mean something like love. In tinh, you find elements of passion. It can be very deep, absorbing the whole of your being. Nghiã is a kind of continuation of tinh. With nghiã you feel much calmer, more understanding, more willing to sacrifice to make the other person happy, and more faithful. You are not as passionate as in tinh, but your love is deeper and more solid. Nghiã will keep you and the other person together for a long time. It is the result of living together and sharing difficulties and joy over time.

You begin with passion, but, living with each other, you encounter difficulties, and as you learn to deal with them, your love deepens. Although the passion diminishes, nghiã increases all the time. Nghiã is a deeper love, with more wisdom, more interbeing, more unity. You understand the other person better. You and that person become one reality. Nghiã is like a fruit that is already ripe. It does not taste sour anymore; it is only sweet.

In nghiã, you feel gratitude for the other person. "Thank you for having chosen me. Thank you for being my husband or my wife. There are so many people in society, why have you chosen me? I am very thankful." That is the beginning of nghiã, the sense of thankfulness for your having chosen me as your companion to share the best things in yourself, as well as your suffering and your happiness.

When we live together, we support each other. We begin to understand each other's feelings and difficulties. When the other person has shown his or her understanding of our problems, difficulties, and deep aspirations, we feel thankful for that understanding. When you feel understood by someone, you stop being unhappy. Happiness is, first of all, feeling understood. "I am grateful because you have proved that you understand me. While I was having difficulty and remained awake deep into the night, you took care of me. You showed me that my well-being is your own well-being. You did the impossible in order to bring about my well-being. You took care of me in a way that no one else in this world could have. For that I am grateful to you."

If the couple lives with each other for a long time, "until our hair becomes white and our teeth fall out," it is because of nghiã, and not because of tinh. Tinh is passionate love. Nghiã is the kind of love that has a lot of understanding and gratitude in it.

All love may begin by being passionate, especially for younger people. But in the process of living together, they have to learn and practice love, so that selfishness—the tendency to possess—will diminish, and the elements of understanding and gratitude will settle in, little by little, until their love becomes nourishing, protecting, and reassuring. With nghiã, you are very sure that the other person will take care of you and will love you until your teeth fall out and your hair becomes white. Nothing will assure you that the person will be with you for a long time except nghiã. Nghiã is built by both of you in your daily life.

To meditate is to look into the nature of our love to see the kind of elements that are in it. We cannot call our love just tinh or nghiã, possessive love or altruistic love, because there may be elements of both in it. It may be ninety percent possessive love, three percent altruistic love, two percent gratitude, and so on. Look deeply into the nature of your love and find out. The happiness of the other person and your own happiness depend on the nature of your love. Of course you have love in you, but what is important is the nature of that love. If you realize that there is a lot of maitri

and karuna in your love, that will be very reassuring. Nghiã
will be strong in it.

Children, if they observe deeply, will see that what keeps
their parents together is nghiã and not passionate love. If
their parents take good care of each other, look after each
other with calmness, tenderness, and care, nghiã is the foundation of that care. That is the kind of love we really need
for our family and for our society.

In practicing the Third Mindfulness Training, we should
always look into the nature of our love in order to see and
not be fooled by our feelings. Sometimes we feel that we
have love for the other person, but maybe that love is only
an attempt to satisfy our own egoistic needs. Maybe we have
not looked deeply enough to see the needs of the other
person, including the need to be safe, protected. If we have
that kind of breakthrough, we will realize that the other
person needs our protection, and therefore we cannot look
upon him or her just as an object of our desire. The other
person should not be looked upon as a kind of commercial
item.

Sex is used in our society as a means for selling products.
We also have the sex industry. If we don't look at the other
person as a human being, with the capacity of becoming a
Buddha, we risk transgressing this mindfulness training.
Therefore the practice of looking deeply into the nature
of our love has a lot to do with the practice of the Third
Mindfulness Training.

*"I will do everything in my power to protect children from
sexual abuse and to prevent couples and families from being broken by sexual misconduct."* Adults who were molested as

children continue to suffer very much. Everything they think, do, and say bears the mark of that wound. They want to transform themselves and heal their wound, and the best way to do this is to observe the Third Mindfulness Training. Because of their own experience, they can say, "As a victim of sexual abuse, I vow to protect all children and adults from sexual abuse." Our suffering becomes a kind of positive energy that will help us become a bodhisattva. We vow to protect all children and other people. And we *also* vow to help those who abuse children sexually, because they are sick and need our help. The ones who made us suffer become the object of our love and protection. The ones who will molest children in the future become the objects of our love and protection.

We see that until the sick people are protected and helped, children are going to continue to be abused sexually. We vow to help these people so that they will not molest children any longer. At the same time, we vow to help children. We take not only the side of children who are being molested, but the other side also. These molesters are sick, the products of an unstable society. They may be an uncle, an aunt, a grandparent, or a parent. They need to be observed, helped, and, if possible, healed. When we are determined to observe this mindfulness training, the energy that is born helps us transform into a bodhisattva, and that transformation may heal us even before we begin to practice. The best way for anyone who was molested as a child to heal is to take this mindfulness training and vow to protect children and adults who may be sick, who may be repeating the kind of destructive actions that will cause a child to be wounded for the rest of his or her life.

Deep Listening and Loving Speech

Aware of the suffering caused by unmindful speech and the inability to listen to others, I am committed to cultivating loving speech and deep listening in order to bring joy and happiness to others and relieve others of their suffering. Knowing that words can create happiness or suffering, I am determined to speak truthfully, with words that inspire self-confidence, joy, and hope. I will not spread news that I do not know to be certain and will not criticize or condemn things of which I am not sure. I will refrain from uttering words that can cause division or discord, or that can cause the family or the community to break. I am determined to make all efforts to reconcile and resolve all conflicts, however small.

There is a saying in Vietnamese, "It doesn't cost anything to have loving speech." We only need to choose our words carefully, and we can make other people happy. To use words mindfully, with loving kindness, is to practice generosity. Therefore this training is linked directly to the Second Mindfulness Training. We can make many people happy just by practicing loving speech. Again, we see the interbeing nature of the Five Mindfulness Trainings.

Many people think they will be able to practice generosity only after they have accumulated a small fortune. I know young people who dream of getting rich so they can bring happiness to others: "I want to become a doctor or the president of a big company so I can make a lot of money and help many people." They do not realize that it is often more difficult to practice generosity after you are wealthy. If you are motivated by loving kindness and compassion, there are many ways to bring happiness to others right now, starting with kind speech. The way you speak to others can offer them joy, happiness, self-confidence, hope, trust, and enlightenment. Mindful speaking is a deep practice.

Avalokitesvara Bodhisattva is a person who has learned the art of listening and speaking deeply in order to help people let go of their fear, misery, and despair. He is the model of this practice, and the door he opens is called the "universal door." If we practice listening and speaking according to Avalokitesvara, we too will be able to open the universal door and bring joy, peace, and happiness to many people and alleviate their suffering.

> The universal door manifests itself
> in the voice of the rolling tide.
> Hearing and practicing it, we become a child,
> born from the heart of a lotus,
> fresh, pure, and happy,
> capable of speaking and listening
> in accord with the universal door.
> With only one drop of the water
> of compassion
> from the branch of the willow,
> spring returns to the great Earth.

I learned this beautiful poem when I studied the *Lotus Sutra* at age sixteen. When you hear "the voice of the rolling tide," which is Avalokitesvara's practice, symbolizing the universal door, you are transformed into a child born in the heart of a lotus. With only one drop of the water of compassion from the willow branch of the bodhisattva, spring returns to our dry Earth. The dry Earth means the world of suffering and misery. The drop of compassionate water is the practice of loving kindness, symbolized by the water on the willow branch. Avalokitesvara is described by the Chinese, Vietnamese, Koreans, and Japanese as the person holding the willow branch. He dips the branch into the water of compassion of his heart, and wherever he sprinkles that water, everything is reborn. When he sprinkles it on dry, dead branches, they turn green. Dead branches also symbolize suffering and despair, and green vegetation symbolizes the return of peace and happiness. With only one drop of that water, spring returns to our great Earth.

In the "Universal Door" chapter of the *Lotus Sutra,* Avalokitesvara's voice is described in five ways: the wondrous voice, the voice of the world regarded, the *brahma* voice, the voice of the rising tide, and the voice of world surpassing. We should always keep these five voices in mind.

First, there is the wondrous voice. This is the kind of speaking that will open the universal door and make everything possible again. This voice is pleasant to hear. It is refreshing and brings calm, comfort, and healing to our soul. Its essence is compassion.

Second, there is the voice of the world regarded. The meaning of the word Avalokitesvara is "the one who looks deeply into the world and hears the cries of the world." This voice relieves our suffering and suppressed feelings, because it is the voice of someone who understands us deeply—our anguish, despair, and fear. When we feel understood, we suffer much less.

Third, there is the brahma voice. Brahma means noble—not just the ordinary voice of people, but the noble speech that springs forth from the willingness to bring happiness and remove suffering. Love, compassion, joy, and equanimity are the *Four Brahmaviharas*, noble dwellings of Buddhas and bodhisattvas. If we want to live with Buddhas and bodhisattvas, we can dwell in these mansions.

During the time of the Buddha, the aim of the practice of many people was to be born and to live together with Brahma. It was similar to the Christian practice of wanting to go to Heaven to be with God. "In my Father's house there are many mansions," and you want to live in one of these mansions. For those who wanted to be with Brahma, the Buddha said, "Practice the four noble dwellings: love, compassion, joy, and equanimity." If we want to share one teaching of the Buddha with our Christian friends, it would be the same: "God is love, compassion, joy, and impartiality." If you want to be with God, practice these four dwellings. If you don't practice these four, no matter how much you pray or talk about being with God, going to Heaven will not be possible.

Fourth, the voice of the rising tide is the voice of the Buddhadharma. It is a powerful voice, the kind of voice that silences all wrong views and speculations. It is the lion's roar that brings absolute silence to the mountain and brings about transformation and healing.

Fifth, the voice of the world surpassing is the voice with which nothing can be compared. This voice does not aim at fame, profit, or a competitive edge. It is the thundering silence that shatters all notions and concepts.

The wondrous voice, the voice of the world regarded, the brahma voice, the voice of the rising tide, and the voice of the world surpassing are the voices we are to be mindful of. If we contemplate these five kinds of voices, we assist Avalokitesvara in opening the universal door, the door of real listening and real speaking.

Because he lives a mindful life, always contemplating the world, and because he is the world regarder, Avalokitesvara notices a lot of suffering. He knows that much suffering is born from unmindful speech and the inability to listen to others; therefore he practices mindful, loving speech and listening deeply. Avalokitesvara can be described as the one who teaches us the best way to practice the Fourth Mindfulness Training.

"Aware of the suffering caused by unmindful speech and the inability to listen to others, I am committed to cultivating loving speech and deep listening in order to bring joy and happiness to others and relieve others of their suffering." This is exactly the universal door practiced by Avalokitesvara.

Never in the history of humankind have we had so many means of communication—television, telecommunications, telephones, fax machines, wireless radios, hot lines, and red lines—but we still remain islands. There is so little communication between the members of one family, between the individuals in society, and between nations. We suffer from so many wars and conflicts. We surely have not cultivated the arts of listening and speaking. We do not know how to listen to each other. We have little ability to hold an intelligent or meaningful conversation. The universal door of communication has to be opened again. When we cannot communicate, we get sick, and as our sickness increases, we suffer and spill our suffering on other people. We purchase the services of psychotherapists to listen to our suffering, but if psychotherapists do not practice the universal door, they will not succeed. Psychotherapists are human beings who are subject to suffering like the rest of us. They might have problems with their spouses, children, friends, and society. They also have internal formations. They may have a lot of suffering that cannot be communicated to even the most beloved person in their life. How can they sit there and listen to our suffering, and understand our suffering? Psychotherapists have to practice the universal door, the Fourth Mindfulness Training—deep listening and mindful speech.

Unless we look deeply into ourselves, this practice will not be easy. If there is a lot of suffering in you, it is difficult to listen to other people or to say nice things to them. First you have to look deeply into the nature of your anger, despair, and suffering to free yourself, so you can be available to others. Suppose your husband said something unkind on Monday and it hurt you. He used unmindful speech and does not have the ability to listen. If you reply right away out of your anger and suffering, you risk hurting him and making his suffering deeper. What should you do? If you suppress your anger or remain silent, that can hurt you, because if you try to suppress the anger in you, you are suppressing yourself. You will suffer later, and your suffering will bring more suffering to your partner.

into it, and you would like him to look deeply into it also. Then you can make an appointment for Friday evening to look at it together. One person looking at the roots of your suffering is good, two people looking at it is better, and two people looking together is best.

I propose Friday evening for two reasons. First, you are still angry, and if you began discussing it now, it may be too risky. You might say things that will make the situation worse. From now until Friday evening, you can practice looking deeply into the nature of your anger, and the other person can also. While driving the car, he might ask himself, "What is so serious? Why did she get so upset? There must be a reason." While driving, you will also have a chance to look deeply into it. Before Friday night, one or both of you may see the root of the problem and be able to tell the other and apologize. Then on Friday night, you can have a cup of tea together and enjoy each other. If you make an appointment, you will both have time to calm down and look deeply. This is the practice of meditation. Meditation is to calm ourselves and to look deeply into the nature of our suffering.

When Friday night comes, if the suffering has not been transformed, you will be able to practice the art of Avalo-kitesvara. You sit together and practice deep listening—one person expressing herself, while the other person listens deeply. When you speak, you tell the deepest kind of truth, and you practice loving speech. Only by using that kind of speech will there be a chance for the other person to understand and accept. While listening, you know that only with deep listening can you relieve the suffering of the other person. If you listen with just half an ear, you cannot do it. Your presence must be deep and real. Your listening must be of a good quality in order to relieve the other person of his suffering. This is the practice of the Fourth Mindfulness Training. The second reason for waiting until Friday is that when you neutralize that feeling on Friday evening, you have Saturday and Sunday to enjoy being together.

Suppose you have some kind of internal formation regarding a member of your family or community, and you don't feel joyful being with that person. You can talk to her about simple things, but you don't feel comfortable talking with her about anything deep. Then one day, while doing housework, you notice that the other person is not doing anything at all, is not sharing the work that needs to be done, and you begin to feel uneasy. "Why am I doing so much and she isn't doing anything? She should be working." Because of this comparison, you lose your happiness. But instead of telling the other person, "Please, Sister, come and help with the work," you say to yourself, "She is an adult. Why should I have to say something to her? She should be more responsible!" You think that way because you already have some internal formation about the other person. The shortest way is always the direct way. "B" can go to "A" and say, "Sister, please come and help." But you do not do that. You keep it to yourself and blame the other person.

The next time the same thing happens, your feeling is even more intense. Your internal formation grows little by little, until you suffer so much that you need to talk about it with a third person. You are looking for sympathy in order to share the suffering. So, instead of talking directly to "A," you talk to "C." You look for "C" because you think that "C" is an ally who will agree that "A" is not behaving well at all.

If you are "C," what should you do? If you already have some internal formations concerning "A," you will probably be glad to hear that someone else feels the same. Talking to each other may make you feel better. You are becoming allies — "B" and "C" against "A." Suddenly "B" and "C" feel close to each other, and both of you feel some distance from "A." "A" will notice that.

"A" may be very nice. She would be capable of responding directly to "B" if "B" could express her feelings to her. But "A" does not know about "B's" resentment. She just feels some kind of cooling down between herself and "B," without knowing why. She notices that "B" and "C" are becoming close, while both of them look at her coldly. So she thinks, "If they don't want me, I don't need them." She steps farther back from them, and the situation worsens. A triangle has been set up.

If I were "C," first of all, I would listen to "B" attentively, understanding that "B" needs to share her suffering. Knowing that the direct way is the shortest way, I would encourage "B" to speak directly to "A." If "B" is unable to do this, I would offer to speak to "A" on "B's" behalf, either with "B" present, or alone.

But, most important, I would not transmit to anyone else what "B" tells me in confidence. If I am not mindful, I may tell others what I now know about "B's" feelings, and soon the family or the community will be a mess. If I do these things — encourage "B" to speak directly with "A" or speak with "A" on "B's" behalf, and not tell anyone else what "B" has told me—I will be able to break the triangle. This may help solve the problem, and bring peace and joy back into the family, the community, and the society.

If, in the community, you see that someone is having difficulty with someone else, you have to help right away. The longer things drag on, the more difficult they are to solve. The best way to help is to practice mindful speech and deep listening. The Fourth Mindfulness Training can bring peace, understanding, and happiness to people. The universal door is a wonderful door. You will be reborn in a lotus flower and help others, including your family, your community, and your society, be born there also.

Speech can be constructive or destructive. Mindful speaking can bring real happiness; unmindful speech can kill. When someone tells us something that makes us healthy and happy, that is the greatest gift he or she can give. Sometimes, someone says something to us that is so cruel and distressing that we want to go and commit suicide; we lose all hope, all our *joie de vivre*.

People kill because of speech. When you fanatically advocate an ideology, saying that this way of thinking or organizing society is the best, then if anyone stands in your way, you have to suppress or eliminate him. This is very much linked with the First Mindfulness Training—that kind of speech can kill not only one person, but many. When you believe in something that strongly, you can put millions of people into gas chambers. When you use speech to promote an ideology, urging people to kill in order to protect and promote your ideology, you can kill many millions. The First and Fourth of the Five Wonderful Mindfulness Trainings inter-are.

The Fourth Mindfulness Training is also linked to the Second Mindfulness Training, on stealing. Just as there is a "sex industry," there is also a "lying industry." Many people have to lie in order to succeed as politicians, or salespersons. A corporate director of communications told me that if he were allowed to tell the truth about his company's products, people would not buy them. He says positive things about the products that he knows are not true, and he refrains from speaking about the negative effects of the products. He knows he is lying, and he feels terrible about it. So many people are caught in similar situations. In politics also, people lie to get votes. That is why we can speak of a "lying industry."

This training is also linked with the Third Mindfulness Training. When someone says, "I love you," it may be a lie. It may just be an expression of desire. And so much advertising is linked with sex.

In the Buddhist tradition, the Fourth Mindfulness Training is always described as refraining from these four actions:

1. Not telling the truth. If it's black, you say it's white.
2. Exaggerating. You make something up, or describe something as more beautiful than it actually is, or as ugly when it is not so ugly.
3. Forked tongue. You go to one person and say one thing and then you go to another person and say the opposite.
4. Filthy language. You insult or abuse people.

"I am determined to speak truthfully, with words that inspire self-confidence, joy, and hope." This must be practiced with children. If you tell children they are good-for-nothing, they will suffer in the future. Always emphasize the positive, hopeful things with your children, and also with your spouse.

"I will not spread news that I do not know to be certain and will not criticize or condemn things of which I am not sure. I will refrain from uttering words that can cause division or discord, or that can cause the family or the community to break. I am determined to make all efforts to reconcile and resolve all conflicts, however small."

Reconciliation is a deep practice that we can do with our listening and our mindful speech. To reconcile means to bring peace and happiness to nations, people, and members of our family. This is the work of a bodhisattva. In order to reconcile, you have to possess the art of deep listening, and you also have to master the art of loving speech. You have to refrain from aligning yourself with one party so that you are able to understand both parties. This is a difficult practice.

During the war in Vietnam, we tried to practice this. We tried not to align ourselves with either of the warring parties, the communists or the anticommunists. You will be able to help only if you stand above the conflict and see both the good and bad aspects of both sides. Doing this, you put yourself in a dangerous situation, because you may be hated by both sides. One side suspects that you are an instrument of the other side, and the other side suspects you are an instrument of the first side. You may be killed by both sides

at the same time. That is exactly what many Buddhists in
Vietnam suffered during the war. We did not align ourselves
with the communists, but we did not align ourselves with
the pro-American side either. We just wanted to be ourselves. We did not want any killing; we only wanted reconciliation. One side said that you cannot reconcile with the
pro-Americans. The other side said that you cannot reconcile with the communists. If we had listened to both sides
it would have been impossible to reconcile with anyone.

We trained social workers to go into the rural areas to
help with health, economic, and educational problems, and
we were suspected by both sides. Our work of reconciliation was not just the work of speaking, but also of acting.
We tried to help the peasants find hope. We helped many
refugees settle in new villages. We helped sponsor more
than ten thousand orphans. We helped the peasants rebuild
their destroyed villages. The work of reconciliation is not
just diplomatic; it is concrete. At the same time, we were
voicing the peace in our hearts. We said the people in one
family must look upon each other as brothers and sisters and
accept each other. They should not kill each other because
of any ideology. That message was not at all popular in the
situation of war.

My writings were censored by both sides. My poetry was
seized by both sides. My friends printed one of my poetry
books underground because the Saigon government would
not allow its publication. Then the communist side attacked
it on the radio saying that it was harmful to the struggle,
probably motivated by the CIA. Nationalist policemen went
into bookshops and confiscated the poems. In Huê, one kind

policeman went into a Buddhist bookshop and said that this book should not be displayed; it should be hidden and given out only when someone asked for it. We were suppressed not only in our attempts to voice our concerns and propose ways to settle the problems between brothers and sisters, but also in our attempts to help people. Many of our social workers were killed and kidnapped by both sides. Each side suspected we were working for the other side. Some of our workers were assassinated by fanatic Catholics who suspected us of working for the communists, and some of our workers were taken away by the communist side. Our workers were quite popular in the countryside. They were very dedicated young men and women, including many young monks and nuns. They did not have salaries; they just wanted to serve and to practice Buddhism. In the situation of war, they brought their loving kindness, compassion, and good work, and received a small stipend to live. They went to the countryside without hoping for anything in return.

I remember a young man named An who specialized in helping peasants learn modern methods of raising chickens. He taught them disease prevention techniques. He was asked by a farmer, "How much do you earn from the government each month?" An said, "We don't earn anything from the government. In fact we are not from the government, we are from the temple. We are sent by the Buddhist temple to help you." An did not tell the farmer, who was not so sophisticated, that he was associated with the School of Youth for Social Service, founded by the Department of Social Work of the Unified Buddhist Church. That was too complicated, so he only said that he was sent by the temple.

"Why have you come here from the temple?"

An said, "We are performing merit." This is a very popular term in Buddhism.

The farmer was surprised. He said, "I have learned that in order to perform merit people go to the temple. Now why are you performing merit here?"

The young man said, "You know, my Uncle, during these times the people suffer so much that even the Buddha has to come out here to help. We students of the Buddha are performing merit right here, where you suffer." That statement became the ground of our philosophy of social service, engaged Buddhism. The Buddha has to be in society. He cannot remain in the temple any longer, because people are suffering too much.

In a few years, we became very popular in the countryside of Vietnam. We did not have a lot of money, but because we worked in the way of performing merit, we were loved by the people. The communist side knew that and did not want us to be there, so they came to us during the night and asked who had given us permission to work there. Our workers said that we did not have permission from either the government or the communist side. We were just performing merit here. One time the communists gave the order for our social workers to evacuate an area, saying, "We will not be responsible for your safety if you stay beyond twenty-four hours." Another time, some fanatics came from the government, unofficially, and asked our social workers if they were really social workers from the Buddhist community. Then they brought five of the students to the riverbank, and, after checking once more to be sure that they were Buddhist social workers, said, "We are sorry, but we have to kill you." They shot all five of them. We were suppressed by both sides during the night. They knew that if they suppressed us during the day, the peasants in the countryside would disapprove.

One grenade thrown into my room was deflected by a curtain. Another night, many grenades were thrown into our School's dormitories, killing two young workers, and injuring many others. One young man was paralyzed, and later treated in Germany. One young lady got more than 1,000 pieces of shrapnel in her body. She lost a lot of blood, and was saved by a Japanese friend who was helping us. Later, we were able to bring her to Japan for surgery. They tried to remove the small metal pieces, but 300 pieces that could not be taken out were left in her body.

One day when I was in Paris as representative of the Vietnamese Buddhist Peace Delegation, to be present at the Paris Peace Talks, I received a phone message from Saigon telling me that four social workers had just been shot and killed. I cried. It was I who had asked them to come and be trained as social workers. A friend who was there with me, said, "Thây, you are a kind of general leading a nonviolent army, and when your army is working for love and reconciliation, there surely will be casualties. There is no need to cry."

I said, "I am not a general. I am a human being. I need to cry." Six months later, I wrote a play about the deaths of these students, entitled, *The Path of Return Continues the Journey.**

---

* See *Love in Action: Writings on Nonviolent Social Change* (Berkeley: Parallax Press, 1993).

The work of reconciliation is not diplomatic work alone. It is not because you travel and meet with dozens of foreign ministers that you do the work of reconciliation. You have to use your body, your time, and your life to do the work of reconciliation. You do it in many ways, and you can be suppressed by the people you are trying to help. You have to listen and understand the suffering of one side, and then go and listen to the suffering of the other side. Then you will be able to tell each side, in turn, about the suffering being endured by the other side. That kind of work is crucial, and it takes courage. We need many people who have the capacity of listening, in South Africa, in the Middle East, in Eastern Europe, and elsewhere.

The Fourth Mindfulness Training is a bodhisattva training. We need deep study to be able to practice it well, within ourselves, our families, our communities, our society, and the world.

Diet for a Mindful Society

Aware of the suffering caused by unmindful consumption, I am committed to cultivating good health, both physical and mental, for myself, my family, and my society by practicing mindful eating, drinking, and consuming. I will ingest only items that preserve peace, well-being, and joy in my body, in my consciousness, and in the collective body and consciousness of my family and society. I am determined not to use alcohol or any other intoxicant or to ingest foods or other items that contain toxins, such as certain TV programs, magazines, books, films, and conversations. I am aware that to damage my body or my consciousness with these poisons is to betray my ancestors, my parents, my society, and future generations. I will work to transform violence, fear, anger, and confusion in myself and in society by practicing a diet for myself and for society. I understand that a proper diet is crucial for self-transformation and for the transformation of society.

Whenever we take a bath or a shower, we can look at our body and see that it is a gift from our parents and their parents. Even though many of us do not want to have much to do with our parents—they may have hurt us so much—when we look deeply, we see that we cannot drop all identification with them. As we wash each part of our body, we can ask ourselves, "To whom does this body belong? Who has transmitted this body to me? What has been transmitted?" Meditating this way, we will discover that there are three components: the transmitter, that which is transmitted, and the one who receives the transmission. The transmitter is our parents. We are the continuation of our parents and their ancestors. The object of transmission is our body itself. And the one who receives the transmission is us. If we continue to meditate on this, we will see clearly that the transmitter, the object transmitted, and the receiver are one. All three are present in our body. When we are deeply in touch with the present moment, we can see that all our ancestors and all future generations are present in us. Seeing this, we will know what to do and what not to do—for ourselves, our ancestors, our children, and their children.

At first, when you look at your father, you probably do not see that you and your father are one. You may be angry at him for many things. But the moment you understand and love your father, you realize the emptiness of transmission. You realize that to love yourself is to love your father, and to love your father is to love yourself. To keep your body and your consciousness healthy is to do it for your ancestors, your parents, and future generations. You do it for your society and for everyone, not just yourself. The first thing you have to bear in mind is that you are not practicing this as a separate entity. Whatever you ingest, you are doing it for everyone. All of your ancestors and all future generations are ingesting it with you. That is the true meaning of the emptiness of the transmission. The Fifth Mindfulness Training should be practiced in this spirit.

There are people who drink alcohol and get drunk, who destroy their bodies, their families, their society. They should refrain from drinking. But you who have been having a glass of wine every week during the last thirty years without doing any harm to yourself, why should you stop that? What is the use of practicing this mindfulness training if drinking alcohol does not harm you or other people? Although you have not harmed yourself during the last thirty years by drinking just one or two glasses of wine every week, the fact is that it may have an effect on your children, your grandchildren, and your society. We only need to look deeply in order to see it. You are practicing not for yourself alone, but for everyone. Your children might have a propensity for alcoholism and, seeing you drinking wine every week, one of them may become alcoholic in the future. If you abandon your two glasses of wine, it is to show your children, your friends, and your society that your life is not only for yourself. Your life is for your ancestors, future generations, and also your society. To stop drinking two glasses of wine every week is a very deep practice, even if it has not brought you any harm. That is the insight of a bodhisattva who knows that everything she does is done for all her ancestors and future generations. The emptiness of transmission is the basis of the Fifth Mindfulness Training. The use of drugs by so many young people should also be stopped with the same kind of insight.

In modern life, people think that their body belongs to them and they can do anything they want to it. "We have the right to live our own lives." When you make such a declaration, the law supports you. This is one of the manifestations of individualism. But, according to the teaching of emptiness, your body is not yours. Your body belongs to your ancestors, your parents, and future generations. It also belongs to society and to all the other living beings. All of them have come together to bring about the presence of this body—the trees, clouds, everything. To keep your body healthy is to express gratitude to the whole cosmos, to all ancestors, and also not to betray the future generations. We practice this mindfulness training for the whole cosmos, the whole society. If we are healthy, everyone can benefit from it—not only everyone in the society of men and women, but everyone in the society of animals, plants, and minerals. This is a bodhisattva mindfulness training. When we practice the Five Mindfulness Trainings we are already on the path of a bodhisattva.

When we are able to get out of the shell of our small self and see that we are interrelated to everyone and everything, we see that our every act is linked with the whole of humankind, the whole cosmos. To keep yourself healthy is to be kind to your ancestors, your parents, the future generations, and also your society. Health is not only bodily health, but also mental health. The Fifth Mindfulness Training is about health and healing.

"Aware of the suffering caused by unmindful consumption, I am committed to cultivating good health, both physical and mental, for myself, my family, and my society…" Because you are not doing it only for yourself, to stop drinking one or two glasses of wine a week is truly an act of a bodhisattva. You do it for everyone. At a reception, when someone offers you a glass of wine, you can smile and decline, "No, thank you. I do not drink alcohol. I would be grateful if you would bring me a glass of juice or water." You do it gently, with a smile. This is very helpful. You set an example for many

friends, including many children who are present. Although that can be done in a very polite, quiet way, it is truly the act of a bodhisattva, setting an example by your own life.

Everything a mother eats, drinks, worries about, or fears will have an effect on the fetus inside her. Even when the child inside is still tiny, everything is in it. If the mother is not aware of the nature of interbeing, she may cause damage to both herself and her child at the same time. If she drinks alcohol, she will destroy, to some extent, the brain cells in her fetus. Modern research has proven this.

Mindful consumption is the object of this mindfulness training. We are what we consume. If we look deeply into the items that we consume every day, we will come to know our own nature very well. We have to eat, drink, consume, but if we do it unmindfully, we may destroy our bodies and our consciousness, showing ingratitude toward our ancestors, our parents, and future generations.

When we eat mindfully we are in close touch with the food. The food we eat comes to us from nature, from living beings, and from the cosmos. To touch it with our mindfulness is to show our gratitude. Eating in mindfulness can be a great joy. We pick up our food with our fork, look at it for a second before putting it into our mouth, and then chew it carefully and mindfully, at least fifty times. If we practice this, we will be in touch with the entire cosmos.

Being in touch also means knowing whether toxins are present in the food. We can recognize food as healthy or not thanks to our mindfulness. Before eating, members of a family can practice breathing in and out and looking at the food on the table. One person can pronounce the name of each dish, "potatoes," "salad," and so on. Calling something by its name helps us touch it deeply and see its true nature. At the same time, mindfulness reveals to us the presence or absence of toxins in each dish. Children enjoy doing this if we show them how. Mindful eating is a good education. If you practice this way for some time, you will find that you will eat more carefully, and your practice of mindful eating will be an example for others. It is an art to eat in a way that brings mindfulness into our life.

We can have a careful diet for our body, and we can also have a careful diet for our consciousness, our mental health. We need to refrain from ingesting the kinds of intellectual "food" that bring toxins into our consciousness. Some TV programs, for example, educate us and help us to lead a healthier life, and we should make time to watch programs like these. But other programs bring us toxins, and we need to refrain from watching them. This can be a practice for everyone in the family.

We know that smoking cigarettes is not good for our health. We have worked hard to get the manufacturers to print a line on a pack of cigarettes: "WARNING, SMOKING MAY BE HAZARDOUS TO YOUR HEALTH." That is a strong statement, but it was necessary because advertisements to promote smoking are very convincing. They give young people the idea that if they don't smoke, they are not really alive. These advertisements link smoking with nature, springtime, expensive cars, beautiful men and women, and high standards of living. One could believe that if you don't smoke or drink alcohol, you will not have any happiness at all in this life. This kind of advertising is dangerous; it pen-

etrates into our unconscious. There are so many wonderful and healthy things to eat and drink. We have to show
how this kind of propaganda misleads people.

The warning on cigarette packs is not enough. We have
to stand up, write articles, and do whatever we can to step
up campaigns against smoking and drinking alcohol. We are
going in the right direction. At last it is possible to take an
airplane flight without suffering from cigarette smoke. We
have to make more effort in these directions.

I know that drinking wine runs deep in Western culture.
In the ceremony of the Eucharist and the Passover *seder*,
wine is an important element. But I have spoken to priests
and rabbis about this, and they have told me it is possible
to substitute grape juice for the wine. Even if we don't drink
at all, we can still get killed on the streets by a drunk driver.
To persuade one person to refrain from drinking is to make
the world safer for us all.

Sometimes we don't need to eat or drink as much as we
do, but it has become a kind of addiction. We feel so lonely.
Loneliness is one of the afflictions of modern life. It is similar
to the Third and Fourth Mindfulness Trainings — we feel
lonely, so we engage in conversation, or even in a sexual
relationship, hoping that the feeling of loneliness will go
away. Drinking and eating can also be the result of loneliness. You want to drink or overeat in order to forget your
loneliness, but what you eat may bring toxins into your
body. When you are lonely, you open the refrigerator, watch
TV, read magazines or novels, or pick up the telephone to
talk. But unmindful consumption always makes things
worse.

There may be a lot of violence, hatred, and fear in a film. If we spend one hour looking at that film, we will water the seeds of violence, hatred, and fear in us. We do that, and we let our children do that, too. Therefore we should have a family meeting to discuss an intelligent policy concerning television watching. We may have to label our TV sets the same way we have labelled cigarettes: "WARNING: WATCHING TELEVISION CAN BE HAZARDOUS TO YOUR HEALTH." That is the truth. Some children have joined gangs, and many more are very violent, partly because they have seen a lot of violence on television. We must have an intelligent policy concerning the use of television in our family.

We should arrange our schedules so that our family has time to benefit from the many healthy and beautiful programs on TV. We do not have to destroy our television set; we only have to use it with wisdom and mindfulness. This can be discussed among the family and the community. There are a number of things we can do, such as asking the TV stations to establish healthier programming, or suggesting to manufacturers to offer television sets that receive only stations that broadcast healthy, educational programs, like PBS. During the war in Vietnam, the American army dropped hundreds of thousands of radio sets in the jungles that could receive only one station, the one that made propaganda for the anticommunist side. This is not psychological warfare, but I think many families would welcome a TV set that would allow us to see only healthy programs. I hope you will write to TV manufacturers and TV stations to express your ideas about this.

We need to be protected because the toxins are over-whelming. They are destroying our society, our families, and ourselves. We have to use everything in our power to pro-tect ourselves. Discussions on this subject will bring about important ideas, such as to how to protect ourselves from destructive television broadcasts. We also have to discuss in our families and communities which magazines that we and our children enjoy reading, and we should boycott those magazines that spill toxins into our society. Not only should we refrain from reading them, but we should also make an effort to warn people of the danger of reading and consum-ing these kinds of products. The same is true of books and conversations.

Because we are lonely, we want to have conversations, but our conversations can also bring about a lot of toxins. From time to time, after speaking with someone, we feel paralyzed by what we have just heard. Mindfulness will allow us to stop having the kinds of conversations that bring us more toxins.

Psychotherapists are those who listen deeply to the suf-ferings of their clients. If they do not know how to practice to neutralize and transform the pain and sorrow in them-selves, they will not be able to remain fresh and healthy in order to sustain themselves for a long time.

The exercise I propose has three points: First, look deeply into your body and your consciousness and identify the kinds of toxins that are already in you. We each have to be our own doctor not only for our bodies, but also for our minds. After we identify these toxins, we can try to expel them. One way is to drink a lot of water. Another is to practice massage, to encourage the blood to come to the spot where the toxins are, so the blood can wash them away. A third is to breathe deeply air that is fresh and clean. This brings more oxygen into the blood and helps it expel the toxins in our bodies. There are mechanisms in our bodies that try to neutralize and expel these substances, but our bodies may be too weak to do the job by themselves. While doing these things, we have to stop ingesting more toxins.

At the same time, we look into our consciousness to see what kinds of toxins are already in there. We have a lot of anger, despair, fear, hatred, craving, and jealousy—all these things were described by the Buddha as poisons. The Buddha spoke of the three basic poisons as anger, hatred, and delusion. There are many more than that, and we have to recognize their presence in us. Our happiness depends on our ability to transform them. We have not practiced, and so we have been carried away by our unmindful life-styles. The quality of our life depends very much on the amount of peace and joy that can be found in our bodies and consciousness. If there are too many poisons in our bodies and consciousness, the peace and joy in us will not be strong enough to make us happy. So the first step is to identify and recognize the poisons that are already in us.

The second step of the practice is to be mindful of what we are ingesting into our bodies and consciousness. What kind of toxins am I putting into my body today? What films am I watching today? What book am I reading? What magazine am I looking at? What kind of conversations am I having? Try to recognize the toxins.

The third part of the practice is to prescribe for yourself a kind of diet. Aware of the fact that there are this many toxins in my body and consciousness, aware of the fact that I am ingesting this and that toxin into my body and consciousness every day, making myself sick and causing suffering to my beloved ones, I am determined to prescribe for myself a proper diet. I vow to ingest only items that preserve well-being, peace, and joy in my body and my consciousness. I am determined not to ingest more toxins into my body and consciousness.

Therefore, I will refrain from ingesting into my body and consciousness these things, and I will make a list of them. We know that there are many items that are nutritious, healthy, and delightful that we can consume every day. When we refrain from drinking alcohol, there are so many delicious and wholesome alternatives: fruit juices, teas, mineral waters. We don't have to deprive ourselves of the joys of living, not at all. There are many beautiful, informative, and entertaining programs on television. There are many excellent books and magazines to read. There are many wonderful people and many healthy subjects to talk about. By vowing to consume only items that preserve our well-being, peace, and joy, and the well-being, peace, and joy of our family and society, we need not deprive ourselves of the joys of living. Practicing this third exercise brings us deep peace and joy.

Practicing a diet is the essence of this mindfulness training. Wars and bombs are the products of our consciousness individually and collectively. Our collective consciousness has so much violence, fear, craving, and hatred in it, it can manifest in wars and bombs. The bombs are the product of our fear. Because others have powerful bombs, we try to make bombs even more powerful. Then the other nations hear that we have powerful bombs, and they try to make even more powerful bombs. Removing the bombs is not enough. Even if we could transport all the bombs to a distant planet, we would still not be safe, because the roots of the wars and the bombs are still intact in our collective consciousness. Transforming the toxins in our collective consciousness is the true way to uproot war.

When we saw the video of Rodney King being beaten on the streets of Los Angeles, we did not understand why the five policemen had to beat a defenseless person like that again and again. We saw the violence, hatred, and fear in the policemen. But it is not the problem of the five policemen alone. Their act was the manifestation of our collective consciousness. They are not the only ones who are violent and full of hatred and fear. Most of us are like that. There is so much violence in all big cities, not only Los Angeles, but also San Francisco, New York, Washington, D.C., Chicago, Tokyo, Paris, and elsewhere. Every morning, when going to work, policemen say, "I have to be careful or I may be killed. I will be unable to return to my family." A policeman practices fear every day, and because of that, he may do things that are quite unwise. Sometimes there is no real danger, but because he suspects he may be shot, he takes his gun and shoots first. He may shoot a child playing with a toy gun. One week before Rodney King was beaten, a policewoman in Los Angeles was shot in the face and killed. It is natural that the police in the area became angry when they heard this, and they all went to the funeral to demonstrate their anger and hatred to society and to the administration for not providing them with enough safety. The government is not safe either—presidents and prime ministers get assassinated. Because society is like this, policemen and policewomen are like that. "This is, because that is. This is like this, because that is like that." A violent society creates violent policemen. A fearful society creates fearful policemen. Putting the policemen in jail does not solve the problem. We have to change the society from its roots, which is our collective consciousness, where the root-energies of fear, anger, greed, and hatred lie.

We cannot abolish war with angry demonstrations. We have to practice a diet for ourselves, our families, and our society. We have to do it with everyone else. In order to have healthy TV programs, we have to work with artists, writers, filmmakers, lawyers, and legislators. We have to step up the struggle. Meditation should not be a drug to make us oblivious to our real problems. It should produce awareness in us, and also in our families and in our society. Enlightenment has to be collective for us to achieve results. We have to stop the kinds of consuming that poison our collective consciousness.

I do not see any other way than the practice of these bodhisattva mindfulness trainings. We have to practice them as a society in order to produce the dramatic changes we need. To practice as a society will be possible only if each of us vows to practice as a bodhisattva. The problem is great. It concerns our survival and the survival of our species and our planet. It is not a matter of enjoying one glass of wine. If you stop drinking your glass of wine, you do it for the whole society. We know that the Fifth Mindfulness Training is exactly like the first one. When you practice non-killing and you know how to protect the lives of even small animals, you realize that eating less meat has do with the practice of the mindfulness training. If you are not able to stop eating meat entirely, at least make an effort to reduce eating meat. If you reduce eating meat and drinking alcohol by fifty percent, you will already be performing a miracle; that alone can solve the problem of hunger in the Third World. Practicing the mindfulness trainings is to make progress every day. That is why during the mindfulness training recitation ceremony, we always answer the question of whether we have made an effort to study and practice the mindfulness training by deep breathing. That is the best answer. Deep breathing means that I have made some effort, but I can do better.

The Fifth Mindfulness Training can be like that, too. If you are unable to stop drinking completely, then stop four-fifths, or three-fourths. The difference between the First and the Fifth Mindfulness Training is that alcohol is not the same as meat. Alcohol is addictive. One drop brings about another. That is why you are encouraged to stop even one glass of wine. One glass can bring about a second glass. Although the spirit is the same as the First Mindfulness Training, you are strongly recommended not to take the first glass of wine. When you see that we are in great danger, refraining from the first glass of wine is a manifestation of your enlightenment. You do it for all of us. We have to set an example for our children and our friends. On French television they say, "One glass is all right, but three glasses will bring about destruction." *(Un verre ça va; trois verres bonjour les dégâts.)* They do not say that the first glass brings about the second, and the second brings about the third. They don't say that, because they belong to a civilization of wine. Here in Plum Village, in the Bordeaux region of France, we are surrounded by wine. Many of our neighbors are surprised that we don't profit from being in this area, but we are a pocket of resistance. Please help us.

When I was a novice, I learned that from time to time we had to use alcohol in preparing medicines. There are many kinds of roots and herbs that have to be macerated in alcohol to have an effect. In these instances, alcohol is allowed. When the herbs have been prepared, we put the mixture in a pot and boil them. Then they no longer have an intoxicating effect. If you use some alcohol in cooking, the result may be the same. After the food is cooked, the alcohol in it will not have an intoxicating nature. We should not be narrow-minded about this.

No one can practice the mindfulness trainings perfectly, including the Buddha. The vegetarian dishes that were offered to him were not entirely vegetarian. Boiled vegetables contain dead bacteria. We cannot practice the First Mindfulness Training or any of the mindfulness trainings perfectly. But because of the real danger in our society—alcoholism has destroyed so many families and has brought about much unhappiness—we have to do something. We have to live in a way that will eradicate that kind of damage. That is why even if you can be very healthy with one glass of wine every week, I still urge you with all my strength to abandon that glass of wine.

I would also like to say something about not using drugs. As alcohol has been the plague of one generation, drugs are the plague of another. One young girl in Australia told me that she did not know anyone in her age group who does not take drugs of one kind or another. Often young people who have taken drugs come to meditation centers to deal with the problem of facing life as it is. They are often talented and sensitive people—painters, poets and writers—and by becoming addicted to drugs they have, to a small or large extent, destroyed some brain cells. It means that they now have little stability or staying power, and are prone to sleeplessness and nightmares. We do what we can to encourage them to stay for a course of training in the meditation center, but because they are easily disillusioned, they tend to leave when things become difficult. Those who have been addicted to drugs need discipline. I am not sure that a meditation center like Plum Village is the best place to cure victims of drug addiction. I think that experts and specialists in this field are better equipped than we are. A meditation center should be able to receive educators and specialists in drug addiction as well as the victims of drug addiction for short courses in meditation to make its resources available where they are truly needed.

The practice that we offer is that of the Fifth Mindfulness Training, to prevent someone from becoming involved with drugs in the first place. Parents especially need to know what spiritual food to give their children. So often, children feel spiritually starved by the wholly materialistic outlook of their parents. The parents are unable to transmit to the children the values of their spiritual heritage, and so the children try to find fulfillment in drugs. Drugs seem to be the only solution when teachers and parents are spiritually barren. Young people need to touch the feeling of deep-seated well-being within themselves without having to take drugs, and it is the task of educators to help them find spiritual nourishment and well-being. But if educators have not yet discovered for themselves a source of spiritual nourishment, how can they demonstrate to young people how that nourishment may be found?

The Fifth Mindfulness Training tells us to find wholesome, spiritual nourishment, not only for ourselves but also for our children and future generations. Wholesome, spiritual nourishment can be found in the moon, the spring blossoms, or the eyes of a child. The most basic meditation practices of becoming aware of our bodies, our minds, and our world can lead us into a far more rich and fulfilling state than drugs could ever do. We can celebrate the joys that are available in the simplest pleasures.

The use of alcohol and drugs is causing great damage to our societies and families. Governments work hard to stop the traffic of drugs. They use airplanes, guns, and armies to do so. Most people know how destructive the use of drugs is but they cannot resist, because there is so much pain and loneliness inside them, and the use of alcohol and drugs helps them to forget for a while their deep malaise. Once people get addicted to alcohol and drugs, they might do anything to get the drugs they need—lie, steal, rob, or even kill. To stop the drug traffic is not the best way to prevent people from using drugs. The best way is to practice the Fifth Mindfulness Training and to help others practice.

Consuming mindfully is the intelligent way to stop ingesting toxins into our consciousness and prevent the malaise from becoming overwhelming. Learning the art of touching and ingesting refreshing, nourishing, and healing elements is the way to restore our balance and transform the pain and loneliness that are already in us. To do this, we have to practice together. The practice of mindful consuming should become a national policy. It should be considered true peace education. Parents, teachers, educators, physicians, therapists, lawyers, novelists, reporters, filmmakers, economists, and legislators have to practice together. There must be ways of organizing this kind of practice.

The practice of mindfulness helps us be aware of what is going on. Once we are able to see deeply the suffering and the roots of the suffering, we will be motivated to act, to practice. The energy we need is not fear or anger; it is the energy of understanding and compassion. There is no need to blame or condemn. Those who are destroying themselves, their families, and their society by intoxicating themselves are not doing it intentionally. Their pain and loneliness are overwhelming, and they want to escape. They need to be helped, not punished. Only understanding and compassion on a collective level can liberate us. The practice of the Five Mindfulness Trainings is the practice of mindfulness and compassion. For a future to be possible for our children and their children, we have to practice.

PART TWO

Responses

Jack Kornfield
Maxine Hong Kingston
Annabel Laity
Christopher Reed
Robert Aitken
Patricia Marx Ellsberg
Sulak Sivaraksa
Arthur Waskow
David Steindl-Rast
Gary Snyder
Stephen Batchelor
Joan Halifax
Richard Baker
Chân Không

forget it. There was a cartoon in the *New Yorker* some years ago during the hunting season. One deer turns to the other and says, "Why don't they thin their own goddamn herds?" We get into formulating excuses: "Well, there are too many deer." As we become more conscious and connected with life, it becomes clear that we shouldn't harm others, because it hurts us to kill. And they don't like it; even the tiniest creatures don't wish to die. So in practicing this training we learn to stop creating pain for others and pain for ourselves.

The Second Mindfulness Training asks us to refrain from stealing, meaning not to take what is not ours. Not to steal is called basic non-harming. We need to let go of being greedy and not take too much. More positively, it means to use things with sensitivity and care, to develop our sense of sharing this life, this planet. To live, we need plants, we need animals, and we need insects. This whole world has to share its resources. It is a boat of a certain size with so many beings living on it. We're connected with the bees and the insects and the earthworms. If there weren't earthworms to aerate the soil, and if there weren't bees to pollinate the crops, we'd starve. We need bees, we need insects. We're all interwoven. If we can learn to love the Earth, we can be happy whatever we do, with a happiness born of contentment. This is the source of genuine ecology. It's a source of world peace, when we see that we're not separate from the Earth but that we all come out of it and are connected with one another. From this sense of connectedness we can commit ourselves to share, to live a life of helpfulness and generosity for the world. To cultivate generosity directly is another fundamental part of living a spiritual life. Like the mindfulness trainings and like our inner meditations, generosity can actually be practiced. With practice, its spirit forms our actions, and our hearts will grow stronger and lighter. It can lead us to new levels of letting go and great happiness. The Buddha emphasized the importance of generosity when he said, "If you knew what I know about the power of giving, you would not let a single meal pass without sharing it in some way."

Traditionally there are described three kinds of giving, and we are encouraged to begin developing generosity at whatever level we find it arising in our heart. At first we find tentative giving. This is where we take an object and think, "Well, I'm probably not going to use this anyway. Maybe I should give it away. No, I should save it for next year. No, I'll give it away." Even this level is positive. It creates some joy for us and it helps someone else. It's a sharing and connecting.

The next level of generosity to discover is friendly giving. It's like relating to a brother or sister. "Please share what I have; enjoy this as I do." Sharing openly of our time, our energy, the things we have, feels even better. It's lovely to do. The fact is that we do not need a lot of possessions to be happy. It is our relationship to this changing life that determines our happiness or sorrow. Happiness comes from the heart.

The third level of giving is kingly or queenly giving. It's where we take something — our time or our energy or an object that is the best we have — and give it to someone happily and say, "Please, would you enjoy this too." We give to the other person and take our joy in that sharing. This level of giving is a beautiful thing to learn.

As we start to learn to be more generous, to give more of our time, our energy, our goods, our money, we can find a way to do it not just to fit a self-image or please an external authority, but because it is a source of genuine happiness in our lives. Of course this doesn't mean giving everything away. That would be excessive, because we have to be compassionate and care for ourselves as well. Yet to understand the power of practicing this kind of openness is very special. It is a privilege to be able to bring this generosity into our lives.

The Third Mindfulness Training, to refrain from sexual misconduct, reminds us not to act out of sexual desire in such a way as to cause harm to another. It requires that we be responsible and honest in sexual relations. Sexual energy is very powerful. In these times of rapidly changing relationships and sexual values, we are asked to become conscious of our use of this energy. If we associate this energy in our lives with grasping and greed, exploitation and compulsion, we will perform actions that bring harm to ourselves and others, such as adultery. There is great suffering consequent to these actions and great joy in the simplicity that comes in their absence.

The spirit of this training asks us to look at the motivation behind our actions. To pay attention in this way allows us, as laypeople, to discover how sexuality can be connected to the heart and how it can be an expression of love, caring, and genuine intimacy. We have almost all been fools at some time in our sexual lives, and we have also used sex to try to touch what is beautiful, to touch another person deeply.

Conscious sexuality is an essential part of living a mindful life.

The Fourth Mindfulness Training of conscious conduct is to refrain from false speech. The Eightfold Path calls this right speech. Don't lie, it says. Speak only what is true and useful; speak wisely, responsibly, and appropriately. Right speech really poses a question. It asks us to be aware of how we actually use the energy of our words. We spend much of our lives talking and analyzing and discussing and gossiping and planning. Most of this talk is not very conscious or aware. It is possible to use speech to become awake. We can be mindful of what we are doing when we speak, of what the motivation is and how we are feeling. We can also be mindful in listening. We can align our speech to the principles of what is truthful and what is most kind or helpful. In practicing mindfulness we can begin to understand and discover the power of speech.

Once a master was called to heal a sick child with a few words of prayer. A skeptic in the crowd observed it all and expressed doubts about such a superficial way of healing. The master turned to him and said, "You know nothing of these matters; you are an ignorant fool!" The skeptic became very upset. He turned red and shook with anger. Before he could gather himself to reply, however, the master spoke again, asking, "When one word has the power to make you hot and angry, why should not another word have the power to heal?"

Our speech is powerful. It can be destructive and enlightening, idle gossip or compassionate communication. We are asked to be mindful and let our speech come from the heart.

When we speak what is true and helpful, people are attracted to us. To be mindful and honest makes our minds quieter and more open, our hearts happier and more peaceful.

To refrain from the heedless use of intoxicants is the Fifth Mindfulness Training. It means to avoid taking intoxicants to the point of making the mind cloudy and to devote our lives to developing clarity and alertness. We have just one mind, so we must take care of it. In our country, there are millions of alcoholics and others who have abused drugs. Their unconsciousness and their fearful use of intoxicants have caused great pain to themselves, their families, and all those they touch. To live consciously is not easy—it means we often must face fears and pains that challenge the heart. Abuse of intoxicants is clearly not the way.

I would like to offer some exercises that can help us use the Five Mindfulness Trainings to cultivate and strengthen mindfulness. It is best to choose one of these exercises and work with it meticulously for a week. Then examine the results and choose another for a subsequent week. These practices can help us understand and find ways to work with each training.

1. *Refraining from killing: reverence for life.* Undertake for one week to purposefully bring no harm in thought, word, or deed to any living creature. Particularly, become aware of any living beings in your world (people, animals, even plants) whom you ignore, and cultivate a sense of care and reverence for them too.

2. *Refraining from stealing: care with material goods.* Undertake for one week to act on every single thought of generosity that arises spontaneously in your heart.

3. *Refraining from sexual misconduct: conscious sexuality.* Undertake for one week to observe meticulously how often sexual feelings arise in your consciousness. Each time, note what particular mind states you find associated with them, such as love, tension, compulsion, caring, loneliness, desire for communication, greed, pleasure, aggression, and so forth.

4. *Refraining from false speech: speech from the heart.* Undertake for one week not to gossip (positively or negatively) or speak about anyone you know who is not present with you (any third party).

5. *Refraining from intoxicants to the point of heedlessness.* Undertake for one week or one month to refrain from all intoxicants and addictive substances (such as wine, marijuana, even cigarettes and/or caffeine if you wish). Observe the impulses to use these, and become aware of what is going on in the heart and mind at the time of those impulses.

To enter the human realm, to establish a ground for spiritual life, requires that we bring awareness to all the actions in our world, to our use of intoxicants, our speech, to all of our actions. Establishing a virtuous and harmonious relationship to the world brings ease and lightness to the heart and steadfast clarity to the mind. A foundation of virtue brings great happiness and liberation in itself and is the precondition for wise meditation. With it we can be conscious and not waste the extraordinary opportunity of a human birth, the opportunity to grow in compassion and true understanding in our life.

Home Again
Maxine Hong Kingston

To write out the mindfulness trainings again, we contend with them, and keep them; we build our humanity, and keep our humanity alive. After the Buddha gave the Five Mindfulness Trainings to the world, there have been many editions and translations, trying for language that would enlighten minds in changing times and places. Thich Nhat Hanh has written a strong version; it will inspire us and our difficult end-of-the-Twentieth-Century world. His thinking has gone through fire—war in and outside of Vietnam, the destruction and building of communities, the conditions of life in the East and in the West. These then are the mindfulness trainings of Buddhism as they have evolved through the most exacting tests.

We people who have studied with Thich Nhat Hanh in person and/or through his writing should consider ourselves also authors of this book. Our teacher, Thây, learned from us as we struggled with how to live the trainings. Some of us debated their wording like lawyers (especially arguing over the "Third Precept," its once-wording, "No sex without marriage"); some rebelled at the very idea of rules. In mindful understanding of our complex, modern, American lives, interacting—"interbeing"—with us, Thây has enworded and reworded the mindfulness trainings until they are in their present rigorous form. (In the discussion of the "Third Mindfulness Training," he helps us distinguish between "marriage" and "commitment," the latter having more permanence.) Each training has two parts: "I vow to ... " and "I am determined not to ...." Going beyond what thou shalt not do, we assert positive actions. The doers and authors of these mindfulness trainings — war veterans and peace veterans, men and women, children, citizens of many countries, heterosexuals and homosexuals — are bringing into being through words and deeds a compassionate world community.

Thây has named the trainings "wonderful" — the Five Wonderful Mindfulness Trainings. Wonderful because they have lived for more than 2,500 years, through holocausts and devastations. Wonderful because they are a practicable, useful map and working plan for our lives in the real world. They teach us to effect that world with methods that are reasonable, logical, ethical — no impossible magic here. Wonderful because they can protect us, and show us how to live a joyous life, an interesting, adventurous, deep, large life, and how to be with one another, and with animals, plants, and all the Earth and universe. Wonderful because when we practice the mindfulness trainings, we existentially become humane, we embody loving kindness.

During the 1991 firestorm through the Oakland-Berkeley hills, I stood in the middle of my street, while the houses on either side burned. I was bereft of my house, neighborhood, the book I was writing, and my father, who had died three weeks previously. Suddenly, I felt the emptiness fill with ideas, spirit, history, all that I have thought and lived. Standing in the midst of burning ruins, I was glad that I knew the trainings. Though I kept their tenets imperfectly, even in aspiration I created some invisible good that could not be destroyed. There is an actuality that surrounds and permeates words and things, and exists in their absence. The Five Wonderful Mindfulness Trainings give clear and simple directions to finding that life. In devastation, I have blueprints for making home anew.

The Western Reception of the
Five Mindfulness Trainings
Annabel Laity

Dhyana Master Nhat Hanh has not always transmitted the mindfulness trainings. To transmit the trainings can be seen as a means of taking disciples to oneself. Thich Nhat Hanh has not seen it necessary to have many disciples in that sense. It was only out of a deep conviction that the Five Mindfulness Trainings are what our world desperately needs that he began to encourage meditation students to receive and practice the mindfulness trainings.

When we, his senior students, first began to teach the Five Mindfulness Trainings, because our skill was not equivalent to that of Thây, we met with some resistance. More recently we have not encountered so much resistance, because we have learned to speak more skillfully. The reason for the resistance to the mindfulness trainings among Western students can be worded as follows: "We became students of Buddhist meditation because the religion we received from our parents and teachers did not satisfy us. The ethics of that religion were confined to a series of injunctions—statements of what we were not permitted to do. The people who taught us those ethics were not themselves fully convinced of their deep value but held to them out of fear. We are reasonable, scientific people and do not want to be caught in superstition or fear. We are looking for inner peace and freedom, and to add further injunctions is not what is going to help us go in that direction."

It was incumbent upon us to respond to this resistance. We could see that it was based not so much on what the mindfulness trainings are saying but on a strong reaction to something that seemed to be like the trainings. We needed to go back to the psychology of resistance. So we began by talking about authority, that there is a human need for authority. Authority is someone or something that knows better and can tell us what to do. We invest that authority with a certain amount of power, and then we become afraid of that power. Authority can be either a voice inside us or someone outside us, and there are not many people who do not have recourse to authority of one sort or another. We ask the question: "Is there really any authority apart from our psychological inclination to make one?" Then we see that we are free to make an authority that is beautiful and gives rise to further beauty. We do not create an authority out of fear or by following a tradition blindly. We follow a path that we know from our direct experience brings happiness. Before any ceremony to receive the mindfulness trainings, there is always time for discussion among the meditation students about the trainings. Usually during such a discussion, some opposition to the trainings is voiced. Such a discussion helps meditation students see what is arising for them psychologically in connection with the trainings, and the decision to receive or not receive the mindfulness trainings is made based on listening deeply to what our fellow meditation students have to say from their direct experience.

Buddhism is quite clear that we need to have confidence in our own awakened nature and that this awakened nature belongs to all species. The human awakened nature is the awakened nature that the human being realizes. First of all we touch that awakened nature, just as, when we touch the poet in us, we are inspired to write a poem. The poet in us is part of our awakened nature. The mindfulness trainings are like the beautiful scenery that arouses the awakened nature in us to respond. It is not just a matter of reasoning, although reasoning is certainly there. To receive the mindfulness trainings is the response of our whole being—emotional, rational, and physical.

If the mindfulness trainings are not worded skillfully, they cannot awaken us to respond to them. That is why Dhyana Master Nhat Hanh has taken great care in the presentation of the mindfulness trainings. If you invite guests to your home, you may spend much time arranging the flowers beautifully so that your guests will experience peace and joy when they come. You also become relaxed, because you enjoyed arranging the flowers so much. The flower arrangement of the mindfulness trainings that Thich Nhat Hanh has spent time making for us will bring us great joy, not only at the dinner party (the receiving of the mindfulness trainings) but also in the rest of our lives. Whenever we recite the mindfulness trainings or think deeply about them, their fresh fragrance will enter our hearts, and we will experience another celebration.

Mindfulness Trainings
Are the Whole of the Dharma
Christopher Reed

When we seek to attain freedom in our lives, we often think about "freedom from" rather than "freedom to." The idea of freedom has been something of a cultural obsession in America. We talk of political freedom, economic freedom, religious freedom, freedom of speech… In trying so hard to attain freedom, however, our focus has usually been on what we imagined was restricting us. We don't really have a vision of what freedom actually looks like. We assume that getting what we want, and getting rid of what we don't want, will make us happy. We contrive to remove whatever we think is standing in our way. That we do this without considering the consequences of our actions is borne out by the reports we see in the news every day. Is there no end to our greed? Is there no end to our appalling capacity to cause suffering to others in order to get what we want? It is as though we are still in some collective state of adolescent rebellion. We take up arms, kill, commit rape, destroy species, entire forests, an entire world—rather than listen. Meanwhile, from all around come the words, like an invocation, "It's a free country, I can do what I want!"

It is not surprising that when we first encounter the mindfulness trainings, we see them as limitations. If freedom means doing what we want, then the trainings may well cramp our style.

We have become hypersensitive to anything that threatens to restrict our freedom. The Ten Commandments, we are told, are a gift from a wrathful God who tolerates no argument. The rigidity of hierarchical patterns of thought and institutionalized authoritarianism is the continuing legacy of that gift. The shadow that marches with us is the manifestation of our longing to be rid of it. In the process of trying to find freedom by doing what we want we are in danger of losing everything. To paraphrase the Buddha, "If you think that you will find happiness by getting what you want, you're crazy. You've been doing that all your life and it has never worked." How then can we find a Middle Way between indulgence and restraint?

For a long time, during retreats, we have discussed the mindfulness trainings as a way to make a commitment to cultivate certain positive qualities. Instead of *"Panatipata veramani sikkhapadam samadiyami,"* "I undertake to abstain from taking life," we can say, "I undertake to cultivate boundless compassion towards all beings." This instantly broadens this mindfulness training's application and deepens its meaning. Not only is this mindfulness training now accessible, but no one can sensibly argue with it.

What a continuing delight it is, then, to hear and learn from the new version of the Five Mindfulness Trainings presented by Thich Nhat Hanh: *"Aware of the suffering caused by the destruction of life, I am committed to cultivating compassion....I am determined not to kill, not to let others kill...."*

Instead of, "I undertake the practice to refrain from stealing," Thây says, *"I will practice generosity."* Instead of, "I undertake the practice of refraining from sexual misconduct," he says, *"I am committed to cultivating responsibility."* Instead of, "I undertake the practice of refraining from lying," *"I am committed to cultivating loving speech and deep listening."* Instead of, "I undertake the practice of refraining from using intoxicants," *"I will ingest only items that preserve peace, well-being, and joy."*

In the large collection of Mahayana writings called the *Avatamsaka (Flower Ornament) Sutra* are innumerable expressions of how the entire cosmos interconnects and interpenetrates. One of the ten expressions of interpenetration described there is that all Dharma, all teachings, interpenetrate with all other teachings. How simple, how obvious, that the trainings, the guidelines given to us for living a joyful life, are also an expression of, a doorway into, what is perhaps the deepest expression of the Dharma—mutual causality, interbeing, the infinite causal relations between all things.

"Aware of the suffering caused by exploitation, social injustice, stealing, and oppression, I am committed to cultivating loving kindness and learning ways to work for the well-being of people, animals, plants, and minerals." Because of this, that is. Because I have awareness of certain realities, I cannot but respond in particular ways.

The mindfulness trainings are not just a set of rules. They are an invitation to open up to the promise of who we truly are. The negative, the rule of restraint, takes away from the recognition of our own power to grow. We can heal the wounds of a Puritan tradition. We can undertake the trainings as practice towards something new and wonderful, rather than as a movement away from something we want to avoid, something we may even empower by our denial of it.

The mindfulness trainings are even more than that. They are a way we can define our relationships in the world. We learn to understand responsibility not as duty but as the simple fact of causality. They are an expression of the whole Dharma. Not only is the teaching of mutual causality present in the trainings, but also the teaching of the Four Noble Truths and the Eightfold Path.

As we learn to understand the mindfulness trainings, we come to see them as having many meanings. They are an expression of the many facets of the Dharma. They are also a way to move beyond negativity toward the fulfillment of our practice. They are also voluntary restraints we can take on for ourselves. The word formerly used for "precept" actually comes from roots which mean a notice of warning. When you see a sign that says, *"Danger, don't go here, high voltage,"* you don't ignore it. You don't say that it is negative. You pay attention. The mindfulness trainings are also like that. Don't kill, it's not worth it, don't do it, there are consequences… We come full circle, not back to the mindfulness trainings as negatives, but to the simplicity of an undertaking simply to practice. When the bell sounds, we bow. In the same way, we undertake to cause no harming, to steal nothing.

There is another wonderful aspect to the mindfulness trainings. They are actually impossible to keep! To refrain from harming others? What a profound practice! We receive the Five Mindfulness Trainings knowing that by doing so we are opening up to our own failure. We cannot fix the world, we cannot even fix our own life. By accepting failure we express our willingness to begin again, time after time. By recognizing failure we change, renew, adapt, listen, and grow. It is only by practicing without expectation of success that we can ever truly open to the world, to suffering and to joy. What extraordinary courage there is in risking losing what you know for the sake of the unknown; risking what you think you are capable of for the sake of your true capability! What profound freedom — not having to get it right all the time, not having to live for the sake of appearance! By opening to our own failure, we open to the magnificence of the unknown, participating unconditionally, renewing our life.

Truly, the mindfulness trainings contain the whole of the Dharma.

Precepts and Responsible Practice
Robert Aitken

As Western Buddhists we acknowledge our monastic heritage but tend to consider ourselves beyond that archaic, restrictive, and exclusive way of religious practice. Most of us are not ordained monks or nuns. Our Buddhist centers are not monasteries in any traditional sense. Yet it is our common purpose to carry forward the work of the Buddha Shakyamuni and his Asian successors in our own time and place and cultures. Are we doing it? Is our lay practice a natural outgrowth of the old in new circumstances? Or is there a risk that we might be fabricating something out of contemporary materials that have merely a Buddhist veneer?

We are not the first to struggle with such questions. After Buddhism was introduced to China, the next step was the establishment of monasteries and merit fields of lay devotees—but with a Chinese flavor. The ancient way of life without labor was set aside. "A day without work is a day without eating," Pai chang, the founder of the Ch'an Buddhist monastic system declared. However, it was maintenance work for the most part. *Dana* was and is still the foundation of the East Asian Buddhist institution. The role of laypeople has largely been to support monks or priests and their temples. In Japan, temple membership is made up of *Danka* ("*dana* families").

Layicization has proceeded. To take Japan as an example again, the Kamakura reformation in the thirteenth century shifted responsibility for realizing the Dharma to laypeople to some degree. There has been a general deterioration of the religion during this process, but still one can find ordinary people reciting the Buddha's name or doing *zazen*, consulting with priests about their practice, or taking part in retreats with monks. In new schools of Buddhism, such as the Rissho Koseikai, the leaders are not even ordained and function like Protestant ministers.

In our Western Mahayana centers, monks of both sexes are ordained, though the old rules of celibacy which eroded during earlier reformations are generally not observed. Benedictine rules of work have been applied and some of the centers seek self-sufficiency through business enterprise. Laypeople are in the majority and practice together with ordained monks. Theravada and Vajrayana centers have appeared in the West as well — Theravada with scarcely any deference to the monastic tradition and Vajrayana without much ordination.

It is surely time, high time, for us as Western Buddhists to take stock. To begin with the Buddha's intention: it is clear that he intended the Sangha to be more than a fellowship of people who shared common religious aspirations. As a treasure of the Way, the Sangha for him was the natural grouping that offered the only means for people to find liberation from their anguish. Moreover, the precepts, derived from formulations from the misty past in India and Persia, were for him the comportment of all followers of the Way.

With all the changes in Buddhism, its followers have remained true to this view of the Sangha as the order of Dharma and the precepts as the Sangha mode of life. Still, as a living organism, the Sangha too is evolving. Joanna Macy has shown how Theravada monks in Sri Lanka take their turns with the spade in the Sarvodaya Shramadana, the broadly based village self-sufficiency movement of that country. Lay Western Buddhists expect as a matter of course to take responsibility for their own religious practice.

Thich Nhat Hanh, the "Thây" or "Master" of Vietnamese Buddhism in the West, has given much thought to the Sangha treasure. His Tiep Hien Order includes monks and nuns in Europe and across the world. His peripatetic retreats provide them and lay followers with the kind of Sangha renewal the ancient sages found in their monsoon retreats. As with the original Sangha of the Buddha, the first teaching is the Vinaya, the moral way. His students learn decency with each other, and as decent people set about saving the many beings.

As a foundation for this practice, Thây takes up the *pañca-sila*, the five fundamental precepts of the ancient Way. He frames each of these precepts positively while maintaining their trenchant, negative vigor. His wording is true to the Buddha's profound intention, and, at the same time, it is relevant for modern students who are ready to take full responsibility for their practice. "I vow not to kill" thus becomes: "Aware of the suffering caused by the destruction of life, I vow to cultivate compassion and learn ways to protect the lives of people, animals, plants, and minerals. I am determined not to kill, not to let others kill, and not to condone any act of killing in the world, in my thinking, and in my way of life."

Making this vow our own, we make this way of life our own, modestly assenting, "With all my weaknesses and faults, I accept my role as bodhisattva." The way of the bodhisattva is the practice of "not killing," but what is "not killing" but nurturing life *in fact* with each smile and encouraging word? And what are the other "nots" in the precepts — "not stealing," "not speaking falsely," and so on — but the intimate practice of compassion and protecting people, animals, plants, and minerals! Thây's beautiful words enlarge the scope of the precepts — and this is the goal of most Western teachers, I believe. If in centuries past, the precepts were pro forma pledges or metaphysical formulations, that time has passed. In most of our centers, the precepts are examined in classes or in orientation programs that are required for the Refuge Ceremony. With such study and with the ceremonies themselves comes a clear understanding that we are human whatever our state of realization might be. There is no perfection except the perfection in our hearts which we seek to fulfill as best we can in our families, among our friends and colleagues, and in the world. As teachers and students alike, we take the precepts to heart and apply them in our daily lives as conscientiously as possible — or we are only make-believe Buddhists who can cause widespread harm, as we have seen to our sorrow.

According to the *Avatamsaka Sutra*, when the youth Sudhana entered the magnificent pagoda of Maitreya at the end of his long pilgrimage, he found that it contained an infinite number of pagodas, each of them beautifully adorned. If he entered one of those inner pagodas, he would find that it too contained an infinite number of pagodas. Thus Sudhana realized—made real for himself—the Net of Indra, in which each point is a jewel that perfectly reflects all other jewels. Each being, each element of each being, perfectly includes all others. He came into his own with full awareness, as his own flesh-and-blood treasure of interbeing at last.

Like all folk stories, the sojourn of Sudhana is itself a pagoda to be entered and made real for oneself, as heroine as well as hero, as adult and even elderly, as well as youthful. It is a personalization that is not just a goal that culminates a religious pilgrimage, but it forms the dimension of each step of the way.

This "dimension of each step" is illumined by the precepts of the Buddha. What is "not killing" but the practice of the ultimate intimacy we celebrate in Sudhana, making that intimacy more and more real in fact with each nurturing smile and encouraging word. And what are the other "nots" in the precepts—"not stealing," "not misusing sex," and so on— but Ms. and Mr. Sudhana in this time and place showing their perennial jewels!

And what of the conspiracy of ruin that mocks the metaphors and could bring the *kalpa* of Kuan-yin and Maria and Murasaki and Bach to the flames of total devastation? Somehow we must find expedient means to make real the jeweled network within and alongside consumer exploitation and national interest. This is a step beyond the monastery walls, uncharted by the old teachers. But it is a step, a path, that the unholy alliance of greed, state ego, racism, androcentrism, and technology has made imperative. Not an easy path, certainly. I am grateful to Thich Nhat Hanh for his light and his staff that guide us.

The Five Mindfulness Trainings and Social Change

Patricia Marx Ellsberg

After attending two retreats with Thich Nhat Hanh, I had the feeling of being "in love" with Thây and Sister Chân Không and with a whole community and way of life. And when I vowed to follow the mindfulness trainings, I felt as if I were making a commitment as serious and profound as taking marriage vows.

I have no doubt of the powerful and far-reaching effect the trainings can have on my life if I take them to heart. And yet, during the retreats I found a question persistently recurring as to the relevance of my own personal practice of the mindfulness trainings to social change. In the face of massive violence and injustice in the world, what difference does it make if I follow the trainings, or even if all the thousands of people Thây has touched with his teachings live by them more fully? How would this bring about the radical social transformations that are necessary?

I found myself uncomfortable with what I perceived to be an underlying premise of the retreat: that if enough individuals change, society will change. In my understanding, society is not simply an aggregate of individuals. It is also shaped by social structures and concentrations of power and wealth. There are vested interests that have disproportionate control and work to maintain and profit from inequality and militarism. These forces need to be challenged and transformed before there can be genuine peace or justice.

In a flash of recognition, I saw that many of the policies of my country and those of other nations are based on the flagrant disregard of the trainings. In fact, much of the evil in the world comes from the systematic—and often societally sanctioned—violation of the mindfulness trainings by governments, corporations, and other institutions. Let us measure our own society's conduct by the mindfulness trainings.

The First Mindfulness Training. Think of the Gulf Massacre in this context and the glorification of the slaughter of over a quarter of a million people, many of them civilians. We live in a war economy fueled by a vast military-industrial complex and billions of dollars of arms sales. Our nuclear policy is based on the threat of mass murder, our foreign policy upon institutionalized violence. Our economy depends on the wholesale destruction of nature.

The Second Mindfulness Training. We as Americans comprise six percent of the world's population and consume forty percent of the world's resources. Many of these resources flow to us from countries ruled by dictatorships that our government has installed, supported, and controlled. In turn they set terms of trade favorable to us, while exploiting and terrorizing their own people, with our government's covert support. This amounts to official theft, not "exchange." Most of our military might is used to control what is not rightly ours.

The Third Mindfulness Training. Think of the energy and resources our society devotes to stimulating sexual desire unconnected to commitment or love—through advertising, pornography, and popular culture in general.

The Fourth Mindfulness Training. Governments and politicians lie. The secrecy system exists not so much to keep secrets from the enemy as to keep the truth from the public. Our government routinely resorts to force rather than peaceful means to deal with conflict, while claiming the opposite, as in Panama, Libya, Nicaragua, Grenada, and Iraq.

The Fifth Mindfulness Training. We are constantly bombarded by advertising for alcohol, cigarettes, caffeine, pharmaceutical drugs. Even more pernicious, our government, through its covert intelligence apparatus, is secretly but deeply involved in abetting the operators of the drug trade, as became evident in the Iran-Contra scandal.

Suddenly, during the retreat, I saw a way the trainings can be of utmost social relevance. We must hold them as mindfulness trainings of behavior for nations, institutions, and corporations as well as for individuals. It is essential that we end the double standard that exists between public and private morality. We must ask of our country what we ask of ourselves.

Those of us living in a democracy have a special obligation to do all we can to move our nation along with our own lives in the direction of following the mindfulness trainings. We must act individually and together to prevent the government that represents us from supporting mass murder and terrorism, stealing, lying, supporting drug traffickers, and raping the Earth. In fact, our survival, in the long run, depends on it.

Likewise, the more fully we follow the trainings, the more powerfully we can act for social change. Indeed, political work is an extension of personal life.

In the spirit of Thây's reformulation of the mindfulness trainings in positive terms, imagine a world in which individuals and institutions alike act with compassion and loving kindness, where governments as well as the citizens they serve are mindful, cultivate a healthy environment, and truly protect the lives of people, animals, and plants. Imagine a time when the resources of the Earth are redirected away from killing towards the enrichment of life.

What if our President's policies conformed to Buddhist principles, Americans pledged allegiance to the Five Mindfulness Trainings as well as the flag, and we celebrated Interdependence Day along with the Fourth of July? Such thoughts inspire in me a Buddha smile.

How Societies Can Practice the Mindfulness Trainings
Sulak Sivaraksa

All Buddhists accept the Five Mindfulness Trainings *(pañca-sila)* as their basic ethical guidelines. Using these as a handle, we will know how to deal with many of the real issues of our day.

The First Mindfulness Training is "I vow to refrain from killing." Killing animals and eating meat, for example, may be appropriate for a simple agrarian society or village life, but in industrial societies, meat is treated as just another product, and the mass production of meat is not at all respectful of the lives of animals. If people in meat-eating countries could discourage the breeding of animals for consumption, it would not only be compassionate towards the animals, but also towards those humans living in poverty who need grain to survive. There is enough food in the world to feed us all. Hunger is caused by unequal allocation, and often those who are in need are the food producers.

We must also look at the sales of arms and challenge those structures that are responsible for murder. Killing permeates modern life—wars, racial conflicts, breeding animals to serve human markets, and using harmful insecticides. How can we resist this and help create a nonviolent society? How can the First Mindfulness Training and its ennobling virtues be used to shape a politically just and merciful world? I shall not attempt to answer these questions. I just want to raise them for us to contemplate.

The Second Mindfulness Training is "I vow to refrain from stealing." In the "World-Conqueror Scripture" *(Cakkavatti Sahananda Sutta)*, the Buddha says that once a king allows poverty to arise in his nation, the people will always steal to survive. Right Livelihood is bound up with economic justice. We must take great pains to be sure there are meaningful jobs for everyone who is able to work. We must also take responsibility for the theft implicit in our economic systems. To live a life of Right Livelihood and voluntary simplicity out of compassion for all beings and to renounce fame, profit, and power as life goals are to set oneself against the structural violence of the oppressive status quo. But is it enough to live a life of voluntary simplicity without also working to overturn the structures that force so many people to live in involuntary poverty?

The establishment of a just international economic order is a necessary and interdependent part of building a peaceful world. Violence in all its forms—imperialist, civil, and interpersonal—is underpinned by collective drives for economic resources and political power. People should be encouraged to study and comment on the "New World Order" from a Buddhist perspective, examining appropriate and inappropriate development models, right and wrong consumption, just and unjust marketing, reasonable use and degradation of natural resources, and the ways to cure our world's ills. Where do Buddhists stand when it comes to a new economic ethic on a national and international scale? Many Christian groups have done studies on multinational corporations and international banking. We ought to learn from them and use their findings.

The Third Mindfulness Training is "I vow to refrain from sexual misconduct." Like the other trainings, we must practice this in our own lives, and not exploit or harm others. In addition, we have to look at the structures of male dominance and the exploitation of women worldwide. The structures of patriarchal greed, hatred, and delusion are interrelated with the violence in the world. Modern militarism is also closely associated with patriarchy. Buddhist practice points toward the development of full and balanced human beings, free from the socially-learned "masculine" and "feminine" patterns of thought, speech, and behavior, in touch with both aspects of themselves.

The Fourth Mindfulness Training is "I vow to refrain from using false speech." We need to look closely at the mass media, education, and the patterns of information that condition our understanding of the world. We Buddhists are far behind our Muslim and Christian brothers and sisters in this regard. The Muslim Pesantran educational institutions in Indonesia apply Islamic and traditional principles in a modern setting, teaching their young people the truth about the world and projecting a vision for the future. The Quakers have a practice of "speaking truth to power." It will only be possible to break free of the systematic lying endemic in the status quo if we undertake this truth-speaking collectively.

The dignity of human beings should take precedence over encouraging consumption to the point that people want more than they really need. Using truthfulness as the guideline, research should be conducted at the university level toward curbing political propaganda and commercial advertisements. Without overlooking the precious treasures of free speech and a free press, unless we develop alternatives to the present transmission of lies and exaggerations, we will not be able to overcome the vast indoctrination that is perpetrated in the name of national security and material well-being.

The Fifth Mindfulness Training is "I vow to refrain from taking intoxicants that cloud the mind and to encourage others not to cloud their minds." In Buddhism, a clear mind is a precious gem. We must look within, and truly begin to address the root causes of drug abuse and alcoholism.

At the same time, we must examine the alcohol and drug producing industries to identify their power base. We must overturn the forces that encourage intoxication, alcoholism, and drug addiction. This is a question concerning international justice and peace. Third World farmers grow heroin, coca, coffee, and tobacco because the economic system makes it impossible for them to support themselves growing rice or vegetables. Armed thugs act as their middlemen, and they are frequently ethnic guerrillas, pseudo-political bandits, private armies of right-wing politicians, or revolutionaries of one sort or another. The CIA ran drugs in Vietnam, the Burmese Communist guerrillas run drugs, and South American revolutionaries run drugs. Full-scale wars, such as the Opium War, have been fought by governments wanting to maintain the drug trade. Equally serious is the economic violence of forcing peasants to plant export crops of coffee or tea and the unloading of excess surplus cigarette production onto Third World consumers through intensive advertising campaigns.

Drug abuse and crime are rampant in those cultures that are crippled by the unequal distribution of wealth, unemployment, and alienation from work. Reagan's and Bush's use of the U.S. armed forces to fight the drug trade was, in the end, just as pointless as was Gorbachev's campaign against worker alcoholism; both approaches addressed symptoms, not causes. Buddhism suggests that the only effective solution to these problems can take place in a context of a complete renewal of human values.

These basic ethical teachings apply to us as individuals and as members of society. My thoughts on the Five Mindfulness Trainings and how we might apply them to the situations of the world today are intended only as a first step. I hope discussion of these issues will continue. We need a moral basis for our behavior and our decision-making.

What Is Eco-Kosher?
Arthur Waskow

Over thousands of years, Judaism has evolved a series of teachings intended to govern the Jewish community and to keep it in internal harmony and in harmony with other peoples and the Earth. Twice in Jewish history, profound changes in society have required changes in the content of these teachings in order to achieve a new harmony in the new situation. One of those times was 2,000 years ago, when Hellenism swept across the Mediterranean basin, greatly increasing the ability of human beings to control their own history and the forces of nature, and dispersed the Jewish people into many lands.

The second time is now. Modernity has shattered the Jewish life that had become traditional, has liberated and empowered women, has transformed the very chemistry and biology of the Earth, and threatens to bring about a mass death of many species. Under these conditions, we must reexamine the content of the teachings that sought for harmony under old conditions, while drawing on the wisdom of the entire Jewish past in order to shape the new content.

Part of that wisdom was the code of eating kosher food in which only the meat of non-predatory animals and birds was kosher to eat; the food of mammalian life (milk) and mammalian death (meat) could not be eaten together; even this restricted kind of meat could only be eaten if the animal had been slaughtered in a painless way with prayerful consciousness and ritual; and vegetarianism was viewed as the higher, but not compulsory, path.

Today we must ask ourselves a broader question: Is it food alone that is subject to the teachings of a kosher life-path? If we wish to protect the Earth, then today we must explore a broader set of questions about what might be considered an "eco-kosher" life.

Are tomatoes that have been grown by drenching the earth in pesticides "eco-kosher" to eat at a wedding reception?

Is newsprint that has been made by chopping down an ancient and irreplaceable forest "eco-kosher" to use for a newspaper?

Are windows and doors so carelessly built that the warm air flows out through them and the furnace keeps burning all night "eco-kosher" for a home or a public building?

Is a bank that invests the depositors' money in an oil company that befouls the ocean an "eco-kosher" place to deposit money?

If by "kosher" we mean a broader sense of "good practice" that draws on the deep wellsprings of Jewish wisdom and tradition about protecting the Earth, then none of these ways of behaving is eco-kosher.

"Eco-kosher" might as an approach speak to two kinds of Jews—both those who now live by the traditional code of kosher food and those who have decided the traditional code is no longer important to them. It might speak to other communities as well.

Why does "eco-kosher" transcend these differences? Because the Earth and the human race are in serious danger. Not economic progress but the *way* we have pursued economic progress has brought about this danger. For the sake of our children and our children's children, it is crucial to address the issues. And the Jewish people has its own wisdom on these matters, rooted in our own ancient tradition of ourselves as a pastoral and agricultural people that nourished the Earth, as well as in our modern efforts to nurture the Land of Israel. So it may be of value to the human race to examine and draw on this sense of sacred practicality.

Shabbat—the Sabbath—is the great challenge of the Jewish people to technology run amok. It asserts that although work can be good, it becomes good only when crowned by rest, reflection, re-creation, and renewal. The Sabbaths of the seventh day, the seventh month, the seventh year, and in principle the seventh cycle (the Jubilee at the fiftieth year) give not only human beings but animals and even plants and minerals, the entire Earth, the right to rest.

The modern age has been the greatest triumph of work, technology, in all of human history. This triumph deserves celebration. But instead of pausing to celebrate and reevaluate, we have become addicted to the work itself. For five hundred years, the human race has not made Shabbat, has not paused to reflect and reconsider, to take down this great painting from its easel and catch our breaths before putting up a new canvas to begin a new project.

Torah teaches that if we deny the Earth its Shabbats, the Earth will make Shabbat anyway—through desolation. The

Earth *does* get to rest. Our only choice is whether the rest occurs with joy or disaster.

The Earth and the human race are now faced with such a moment of Shabbat denied. Triumphant human technology, run amok without Shabbat, brings the danger of impending desolation. We can quickly identify several specific areas in which these dangers are already clear:

The multiplication of thousands of nuclear-weapons warheads that, if exploded in a short period, could devastate the planet; the creation from nuclear energy plants of radioactive wastes that will need to be contained and controlled for thousands of years; the galloping destruction of the ozone layer; the overproduction of carbon dioxide from massive deforestations and the extensive burning of fossil fuels, in such a way as to make much more likely a major rise in world temperatures; the destruction of many species through destruction of their habitats.

Torah teaches not that we abandon technology but that we constrain it with Shabbat and all the implications of Shabbat. Instead, we have used technological progress to poison the earth and air and water, so that they poison us with cancer at the very moment when we take in their nourishment.

What we sow is what we reap.

If what we sow is poison, what we reap is also poison.

The planetary biosphere cannot long endure the treatment we are now giving it. Nor can the human race.

Our technology has also transformed the medium of the relationship between Earth and human earthling. Originally, food was the great connection. But that is no longer so. The human race has created an economy in which *energy, minerals,* and *money* take on many of the roles that land and food originally had.

That is why an eco-kosher approach to life requires us to look beyond food to such other consumable items as wood, oil, and aluminum, and to where and how we save and invest our money.

And the new conditions of the planet may also point toward changes in the content of teachings outside the arena of kosher or eco-kosher consuming of goods from the Earth.

The most important of these is the area of population and the sexual ethics that bear on population. Traditionally, Jewish sexual ethics operated under the rubric of "Be fruitful and multiply, and fill up the Earth." It strongly encouraged sexuality that was likely to procreate and rear more children, and frowned both on celibacy and on all sexuality outside a heterosexual marriage, and even then on sexual relations outside the two most fertile weeks of the woman's ovulation cycle. So traditional Jewish sexual teachings opposed gay or lesbian sexuality, masturbation, most forms of birth control, and sexual relations for the sake of loving pleasure between two adult, unmarried people.

But once the Earth is already "filled up" with human beings, where shall we look for a sexual ethic to balance one that is focused on bearing and nurturing children?

In the books of Jewish wisdom, one that looks to such a time is the *Song of Songs.* It celebrates a Garden of Eden that is no longer peopled by a childish human race that is just entering rebellious adolescence, but by adults.

Its sexual ethic is one of loving pleasure and flowing relationship between human beings and each other, and human beings and the Earth. Instead of opposing sexual expression except when it is focused on the bearing or rearing of children, the *Song of Songs* celebrates sexual expression except when it is coerced or demeaning.

In the new era of the Earth, the human race needs to balance a sexual ethic focused on children and the family with one focused on love and joy. The new "eco-kosher" sexual ethic might affirm sexual relationships between adults of any sexual orientation where there is honesty, caring, no coercion or other misuse of an imbalance in power between the parties, and no deceit of others or an attack on other relationships. And it might affirm as well the special relationship of two people who have decided to make a more permanent commitment, including one to have and rear children, so long as they have made a careful judgment in the light of the Earth's needs about how many children will suffice.

Why should the Jewish people and religious community bother to do all this, and why should other communities encourage the Jews to do it? Why is this a Jewish issue and why is it a Jewish-renewal issue? For two reasons:

We must draw on the wisdom, energy, and commitment of all peoples, each of them in the specificity and uniqueness of its own world view, if we are to heal the Earth, nurture all living beings, and protect our children from environmentally caused cancer, famine, and other disasters.

Just as every unique species of plant and animal brings a sacred strand into the sacred web of life, so does the unique wisdom of each human culture. Just as modernity threatens to narrow and crush the diversity of species, so it threatens to narrow and crush the diversity of cultures. Both Jews and others are helping to heal that web of life if they give new heart and new life to endangered cultures as well as endangered species. The Jewish people is one such endangered culture.

The shift from Biblical to Rabbinic Judaism is one of the most useful histories of how a culture can renew and transform itself without losing its own identity. Now when the world is being profoundly transformed, every religious tradition needs to examine how best to renew and transform itself, neither abandoning its own deepest wisdom nor getting stuck in the transient versions of itself that worked in a departed past.

Precepts
David Steindl-Rast

Precepts fascinate me. Not the task of keeping them; that's not what I mean, but their variety throughout the world. The moral precepts of different ages and cultures display a rich texture of human diversity which I find captivating. My thrill reminds me of my mother's button box, when I was five; or of the seashells I bring home from a morning walk on the beach and arrange on the tabletop by size and color and shape. It's a basic human fascination with sameness in difference and difference in sameness.

My friend Graham Carey tapped the source of this thrill when he surprised his children one Christmas with a home-made book, later published as *The Tail Book:* page after page, nothing but animal tails, from fox to lizard, from lion to swallow, from the peacock's fan to our own almost invisible tailbone. Children never fail to find delight in variations. And the child in us never tires of them either, be they Mozart's variations on "Twinkle, Twinkle, Little Star" or Mother Nature's endless variations on the night sky. That's one reason why I find the worldwide diversity of precepts and taboos so thrilling.

The hitchhiker with his skullcap and earlocks whom I took along, one day in New England, nervously eyed the Swiss army knife with which I was about to slice the cheese and apples we shared. What else had I been cutting with this knife? Meat? I admired the mindfulness with which he kept utensils used with milk products separate from those used with meat, following orthodox Jewish precepts. I respected that same mindfulness and dedication when we had to drive fast to get him to a friend's house before sundown, that Friday night, when his Sabbath rest began.

The same preoccupations with keeping precepts struck me on the other side of the world, in New Zealand. Aotearoa, as the Maoris call it, the "Land of the Long White Cloud," is one of the few places where a native population has never been defeated by the white conquerors. *Pakiha* (the whites) live side by side with Maoris, but they are often unaware of their neighbors' taboos. I remember the deep distress of a Maori woman, when her new Pakiha neighbors hung dish towels ("tea towels" they call them down-under) next to T-shirts on the clothesline to dry. Never, never must things that have to do with food come in contact with clothes.

In India, even the best-intentioned tourist may cause an uproar in the crowd by inadvertently walking counterclockwise around a holy image. Turning one's left shoulder towards something sacred would be far worse in Calcutta than offering someone one's left hand for a handshake in London. Of course, the line between sacred precepts and social conventions gets blurred here. Yet these two areas may be more deeply connected than we think. By looking more closely at those precepts, taboos, and conventions that seem arbitrary to us, we may be able to catch sight of something below the surface, a common ground for the great variety of phenomena. By listening closely to the confusing variety of precepts we may begin to hear a theme of which they are variations.

Here we must confront the decisive question: is there a common theme expressed in the dazzling variety of precepts all over the world? My answer is yes, and the theme is a sense of belonging.

We might call it "outlandish," when someone uses the left hand for a handshake instead of the right. Precisely: that's not what one who belongs to our land does. One of our own wouldn't do that. For worshippers in India counterclockwise circumambulation is equally outlandish, but with the added dimension of religious sanction. Every act of worship strengthens the bonds that connect us with the Ultimate. At the same time, it strengthens the bonds that connect us with those who worship as we do. Worship is—according to the root meaning of the word—an expression of reverence for what is most worthy of honor. It is not restricted to a theistic, not even to a narrowly religious context. It gives, on the other hand, religious weight to anything we do with a view to our ultimate values. In this sense, following religious precepts is an act of worship.

For Maoris, their rootedness in tradition is an ultimate value. It connects them with their ancestors and with all that their ancestors held holy—Earth, Sea, and Sky, all creatures who share this world with us, and all the invisible Presences in this Earth home of ours. The keeping of any taboo strengthens the bonds of belonging to that home of all, which Gary Snyder so aptly calls the Earth Household.

Our orthodox Jewish friend has a much smaller community in mind, the narrow circle of those who worship like him. Primarily, however, he doesn't have humans in mind at all, but God. Yet where did he learn God's precepts, if not in a community? And is it not through bonding with that community that he belongs to God? And is not that sense of belonging the bliss he is following through meticulous mindfulness in daily practice? From what seems to others mere social convention, all the way to love of God and neighbor, the precepts are all of one piece for orthodox believers, for they are so many different expressions of ultimate belonging.

With this belonging goes a separation from all those who don't belong. In fact, the many precepts of separating—milk products from meat products, eating from all other body functions, and countless similar taboos in different traditions—all express and emphasize the theme of separating from those who do not belong. This is the shadow of the theme of belonging. The positive theme of every moral code that ever existed could be summarized in the words: this is how one behaves towards those to whom one belongs. Beyond this circle of belonging are the outsiders. Moral code differs from moral code not in its essence, not at all, but only in how exclusively or inclusively we draw the circle of belonging.

We have reached a threshold in human history, today. From now on morality must either be all-inclusive or it becomes immoral. In our world there is no more room for outsiders. And our sense of belonging must include not only humans, but animals, plants, and all the inanimate furniture of our Earth Household. Nothing will do any more, but the widest possible horizon of belonging.

That is why we see two momentous moral changes happening in our time. All precept structures based on exclusiveness are breaking down, belonging to the past. A new appreciation for precepts based on a universal sense of belonging is fast gaining ground, belonging to the future. Of all our religious precepts only those will survive which are the expression of limitless belonging, but those will indeed survive. They will be shaping the future if there is to be a future.

More and more people are beginning to realize that the survival of our planet depends on our sense of belonging — to all other humans, to dolphins caught in dragnets, to chickens and pigs and calves raised in animal concentration camps, to redwoods and rainforests, to kelp beds in our oceans, and to the ozone layer. More and more people are becoming aware that every act that affirms this belonging is a moral act of worship, the fulfillment of a precept written in every human heart.

This is ultimately why precepts fascinate me, those falling into disuse as well as those that will last as long as humans are human: they are variations on one and the same theme, a theme that challenges the human heart anew in every age. What fascinated me at the outset was the amazing diversity of precepts. What thrills me on second thought is the one great challenge that speaks with such diverse tongues, the challenge to say "yes" wholeheartedly, a limitless "yes" to belonging.

Indra's Net as Our Own

Gary Snyder

On the final page of his essay, "Indra's Net as Food Chain — Gary Snyder's Ecological Vision," David Barnhill says: "For Snyder, Indra's net is put into practice in hunting and eating, in which the hunted/eaten shows compassion and the hunter/eater displays purity and respect."[*] I would expand this to say that any kind of gathering or gardening calls for compassion, purity, and respect on all sides: as much mindfulness is asked of the vegetarian as is of the hunter. He goes on to say that "Buddhism, of course, has traditionally prohibited the eating of meat, but we can see why Snyder chooses not to accept that principle." I do, in fact, accept that principle, as an idea, a challenge, and a goal, appropriate to time and place. To choose not to eat meat is a primary extension of the First Precept, *ahimsa*, non-harming, no "unnecessary harm." But this is the *saha*-world of *dukkha*, tragic with suffering, and people live in poverty and necessity, animals and plants live mutually on

---

[*] Published in *The Ten Directions*, Zen Center of Los Angeles, Spring/Summer 1990. Barnhill offers this description of Indra's net: "In order to suggest the nature of this network of interrelationship, Hua Yen developed the image of Indra's net. In this image, the universe is considered to be like a vast web of many-sided and highly polished jewels, each one acting as a multiple mirror. In one sense each jewel is a single entity. But when we look at a jewel, we see nothing but the reflections of other jewels, which themselves are reflections of other jewels, and so on in an endless system of mirroring. Thus in each jewel is the image of the entire net. For Hua Yen, the religious goal is to attain a state of mind that sees the world as interreflective and enables us to live our lives in terms of such a radical interdependence." See also David Barnhill's reply in *Tricycle*, Summer 1993.

each other. It is described in the sutras as the realm of kama, of biological desire and need, which drives everything. Everything that breathes is hungry.

When Barnhill seems to then argue that one *should* thereby eat meat, I must decline to agree. It is Barnhill's conclusion, and not my own, that "if we were to artificially remove ourselves from the meat-eating aspect of our location in the food web … we would seem to be asserting for ourselves a special place in the web." My own opinion is that when and wherever people can live by grains and vegetables alone, it is to be applauded. There are many people for whom this is not a viable option, however. The people of the Arctic are the most obvious case, but also those of the grasslands and deserts, those of the seashore, those of the mountains, have always historically relied on much non-plant food. Most people must have always had to live by a mixed food economy which includes some animal life. Shall we as Buddhists consider them beyond the pale? "Border tribes who cannot grasp the Dharma" (an old Tibetan idea). Surely the bodhisattva spirit does not allow us to reject the other cultures and food-economies of the world out of hand. As for modern food production, although it is clear that the beef economy of the United States and some other countries is a wasteful luxury, it is doubtful that the Third World could get by without cows, chickens, pigs, sheep, and the life of the sea.

The deeper question is one of how we grasp the First Precept. When Oda Sesso, Roshi, my teacher at the Daitokuji *sodo*, came to *Mumonkan* Case 14, "Nansen Kills a Cat," he chose not to sit in the high chair, but sat on the tatami, on the same level as the *unsui.* He said, "This is a case that can be easily misunderstood, and we in Japan have on some occasions perhaps abused it." At the time I thought he was referring to the apparent lack of resistance on the part of the Zen establishment to the emergence of Japanese militarism in the thirties, leading to World War II. Now I think that he was indicating that *anyone* in a discussion that raises the question of deliberately taking life should be sitting right on the floor. One cannot be too humble about this issue. As I listened to his *teisho* back in 1961, I must confess I felt a certain righteousness, because I had been a lifelong pacifist (and on-and-off vegetarian), and thought I knew how to understand the precept. Not so easy.

I had also noticed that even some of the roshis (let alone the monks) ate fish when away from the monastery. One time I was visiting at the temple of a roshi near Mt. Fuji and I asked him, why is it that some priests and monks eat meat or fish? He responded heartily, "A Zen man should be able to eat dogshit and drink kerosene." My own teacher, Oda Roshi, was a strict vegetarian. But he once said to me, "Just because I eat pure food and some of the other priests do not, does not mean that I am superior to them. It is my own way of practice. Others have other ways. Each person must take the First Precept as a deep challenge, and find his own way through life with it."

I am not and never have been what you could call a hunter. I have been a student of hunting and gathering cultures, and have tried to get insight into our fundamental human role from looking at the many millennia of human foraging experience. I have killed a few animals *in extremis* to be sure. On two occasions I put down deer that had been wounded by sport-hunters and wandered in that condition into our part of the forest. When I kept chickens, we maintained the flock, the ecology, and the economy, by eating excess young roosters and, at the other end of the life cycle, stewing an occasional elderly hen. In doing this I experienced the sadness and necessity that envelops the peasant people of the world. They (and I) could not but run their flock this way, for anything else would be a luxury, that is to say uneconomic.

Also, my hen-flock (unlike commercial hens who are tightly caged) got to run wild and scratch all day, had a big rooster boyfriend, and lived the vivid and sociable life of jungle fowl. They were occasionally taken away by bobcats, raccoons, wild dogs, and coyotes. Did I hate the bobcats and coyotes for this? At some times, taking sides with the chickens, I almost did. We must work hard to put aside our own opinions and stand humbly aside as the Great System goes through its moves. I quit keeping chickens because I found it to be noneconomic. Happily loose flocks cannot compete with factory egg production, which reduces hens to machines (but protects them from bobcats). On a deep level I do not think I can approve of the domestication of birds and animals: too much is taken out of their self-sufficient wild natures.

As for venison, for many years several families in this area have carefully salvaged fresh roadkill deer rather than let flesh go to waste. (But then, letting it feed vultures or carrion beetles is no waste.) Where we live, gardening is not so great, but the forest is vast.

The simple distinction "vegetarian/ non-vegetarian" is too simple. Some populations, especially in India and Southeast Asia, are deliberate vegetarians. Most of the rest of the people of the Third World are semi-vegetarians by default. Americans, Australians, New Zealanders, and some Europeans are the large meat consumers of the modern world. In the developed world, vegetarians are usually educated members of a privileged class. Most North American Buddhists have no need to eat meat, and I am not in any way suggesting that they should. They might instead further study their own dependence on fossil fuel economy and an agriculture which produces vegetables and grains in a manner that degrades soil, air, and water, and which endangers the health of underpaid immigrant laborers. Indeed we all need to look for alternative kinds of food production.

My own approach to food is to be curious and grateful. I would like to know where my food came from and who it was, plant or animal. (Okra is a member of the Hibiscus family, originally from Africa! Tomatoes, Tobacco, Potatoes, Eggplant—Nasubi, Brinjal, Aubergine—, and Jimson weed are all Solanaceae together, with those trumpet-shaped flowers. I feel deepened by such facts.) And my family and I say grace and do a little meditation on our food before meals, just as is done on a larger scale in *sesshin* with the meal verses. In the closing section of *The Practice of the Wild*,[*] titled "Grace," I write at some length about "saying grace."

So why, as a practicing Buddhist, have I written poetry and prose about hunters, foragers, and the food chain? Be-

---

[*]   Berkeley: North Point Press, 1992.

cause on a physical level the First Precept is fundamental and our life in regard to food is the first question of economics and ecology. Our food is the field in which we daily explore our "harming" of the world, and how we deal with it. Clearly it will not do to simply stop here and declare that the world is pain and suffering and that we are all deluded. We are called instead to practice. In the course of our practice, we will not transform Reality, but we may transform ourselves. Guilt and self-blame are not the fruit of practice, but we might hope that a *larger view* is. The larger view is one that can acknowledge the simultaneous pain and the beauty of this complexly interrelated real world. It is this realization, in part, that the image of Indra's Net strives to manifest. So far it has been the earlier subsistence cultures of the world, especially the hunters and gatherers, who have—paradoxically—most beautifully expressed their gratitude to the earth and its creatures. As Buddhists we have yet something to learn on that score.

None of what I have been saying is to be seen as rationalization or justification for "breaking" the Precept. As Ryo Imamura recently wrote, "In Buddhism there is no such thing as a 'just' war." If we were to find ourselves going against the precept in some drastic situation and killing or injuring someone else in (say) self-defense, we must not try to justify it. We can only say: This was my decision, I regret that it happened, and I accept whatever results it may entail.

The precept is the Precept, and it stands as a guide, a measure, an ideal, and a koan. It cannot be a literal rule, as if it were one of the Ten Commandments. "Take no life" or "commit no harm" is impossible to totally keep. The Jains of India tried to take ahimsa to its literal (not logical) conclusion, and the purest among them started an institution of starving themselves to death as a moral act. But this is violence against one's own body.

Every living thing impinges on every other living thing. Popular Darwinism, with its emphasis on survival of the fittest, has taken this to mean that nature is a cockpit of competitive bloodshed. "Nature red in tooth and claw" as the Europeans are fond of quoting. This view implicitly elevates human beings to a role of moral superiority over the rest of nature. More recently the science of Ecology, with its demonstrations of co-evolution, symbiosis, mutual aid and support, interrelationship, and interdependence throughout natural systems, has taught us modesty in regard to human specialness. It also has taught us that our understanding of what is and is not "harmful" within the realm of wild nature is so rudimentary that we should not bother to take sides between predators and prey, between primary green producers and detritus-side fungi or parasites, or even between "life" and "death."

Thich Nhat Hanh once said at a gathering of Buddhist Peace Fellowship leaders at Tassajara Zen Mountain Center that we should be grateful for any little appearance of ahimsa wherever it is found in this world. I believe he said that if one officer in a battle leads his troops with a bit more spirit of ahimsa than another, it is to be appreciated. It is my sense of it then, that we must each find our own personal way to practice our precept, within quite a latitude of possibilities, understanding that there will be no complete purity, and in any case, without indulging in self-righteousness. It is truly our "existential koan." This is why I have glossed it, in the Mahayana spirit, as "Commit No Unnecessary Harm."

One can wonder what the practice of ahimsa is like for the bobcat, in the bobcat Buddha-realm. As Dogen says, "Dragons see water as a palace" and for bobcats, the forest is perhaps an elegant *jikido* (dining hall) in which they murmur *gathas* of quiet appreciation to quail, sharing them (in mind) with demons and hungry ghosts. "You who study with Buddhas should not be limited to human views when you are studying water." And what world is it for quail? I only know this: at death, my death and suffering are my own, and I hope I will not blame it on the tiger (or cancer, or whatever) that has brought me down. Of the tiger I would simply ask, "Please, no waste." And maybe growl along with her.

When the single discarded chopstick is found by the Master in the drain, and he scolds the monk, saying, "You have taken the life of this chopstick," we can look at a wasted chopstick, and understand how it has been harmed. Then it should also be said, "You are killing a rainforest," as the use of disposable wood chopsticks in Japan and America in staggering quantities suggests.

Did the Master know the next step? Not entirely. The application of active compassion for creatures in Buddhist China often meant ceremonially releasing caged pigeons and captured fish. Compassion for individual lives is only part of the story. Buddhist China was forced to witness significant species extinction and wholesale deforestation between the fifth and fifteenth centuries. India was vastly deforested well before modern times. Compassion for suffering lives must be enlarged to the scale of a whole watershed, a natural system, a habitat. To save the life of a parrot or monkey is admirable. But unless the forest is saved, they will all die. The whole planet groans under the massive disregard of the precept of ahimsa by the highly organized societies and corporate economies of the world. Thousands of species of animals, and tens of thousands of species of plants, may become extinct in the next century. I hope that readers of this book will see the peace movement, the environmental movement, and our own Buddhist Peace Fellowship in this light, and make the effort to SAVE HABITAT FOR ALL BEINGS a top priority.

The Future Is in Our Hands
Stephen Batchelor

What is your practice?" Many Buddhist practitioners would assume that this question is about the kind of meditation they do, for they tend to answer, "I practice *vipassana*," or "*dzogchen*," or "*shikantaza*." Such responses reflect a widespread view that practice is essentially a matter of spiritual technique. Ethics, from this perspective, is seen as a set of values and precepts that *support* one's practice.

The Buddha, however, spoke of practice *(siksa)* as three-fold: consisting of ethics, meditation, and wisdom. Yet as Buddhists seek to express themselves in the technocentric culture of the West, they often see what they "do" primarily in terms of the second of these three practices, namely meditation. For this fits a worldview in which the solving of problems by means of applying techniques is considered paramount.

The most significant aspect of the emerging engaged Buddhist movement is that of redefining what is meant by "practice." By emphasizing engagement, the focus of practice shifts from an exclusive identification with meditation to an inclusion of ethics. The danger here is that "engaged Buddhists" become subtly (or less than subtly) dismissive of other Buddhists who "only" meditate. As with the technocentrism of meditators, engaged Buddhists are liable to succumb to another Western obsession: the belief that action alone counts.

Ethics as practice begins by including ethical dilemmas in the sphere of meditative awareness—to be mindful of the conflicting impulses that invade consciousness during meditation. Instead of dismissing these as distractions (which would be quite legitimate when cultivating concentration), one recognizes them as potentials for actions that may result in one's own or others' suffering.

The practice of such mindfulness leads to increasing sensitivity regarding the moment-to-moment emergence of thoughts and emotions. Often it is not until I find myself taken over by an emotion, such as anger, that I first become conscious of it. Such meditation trains me to observe states of mind at their inception.

This does not mean that I suppress or disregard those impulses that do not conform to my spiritual self-image. Mindfulness is to accept whatever arises and to recognize it as such. At the root of my practice of ethics is the ability to accept that I am as much a potential murderer, thief, rapist, liar, and drug-abuser as those convicted of such offenses in prison. To practice ethics is to be able to accept the reality of such impulses—and let them go. To let them go means to allow them to follow their own nature of passing away. For only when I affirm an impulse ("Yes, I hate that person!"), do I set in motion the train of events that culminates in verbal or physical action.

As the power of mindfulness increases, it allows me increasing freedom to choose what to do. Mindfulness is empowered, however, not just by a greater capacity to be mindful—we have probably all had the experience of mindfully observing ourselves break a precept. Mindfulness is also empowered by its "sister" qualities of faith, enthusiasm, meditation, and wisdom (the other four of the five powers, *indriya*, the Buddha spoke of). To the extent that such mindfulness is absent, the more a choice is liable to be subject to the forces of psychological habit and social conditioning. Only when mindfulness is fully empowered am I fully free to choose.

What makes me choose one thing as opposed to another? What makes me believe that this action is right while another is wrong? Mindfulness can make me aware of what impulses are arising from moment to moment, but it does not tell me which of these impulses to let go of and which to follow. To know this, I need to be aware of my priorities and values. And such awareness lies at the heart of my Buddhist *faith*.

The practice of Buddhist ethics is grounded in faith. For I can neither prove by logic nor observe through the senses what I regard as right and wrong, good and evil. Even though I may justify my conviction of what is right and wrong by appealing to conscience or intuition or Buddha nature, such an appeal is likewise an act of faith in something (such as conscience) that I can neither prove nor observe.

"Buddhist ethics" generally refers to those sets of precepts that I commit myself to as a layperson, a monastic, an aspiring bodhisattva, a Zen practitioner, or a follower of the Vajrayana. Precepts are formal statements of the values I choose, on faith, to live by. It is to those values, enshrined in the precepts, that I refer when making an ethical choice.

When baldly stated (for example, "Do not kill"), a precept may seem merely to dictate what is forbidden. Underlying this precept, however, are values: that life is precious, that the diminishing of suffering is good, that compassion is good, that the protection and enhancement of life is good.

A tension runs through all the Buddhist traditions between those who emphasize the literal meaning of the precepts and those who emphasize the values that underlie them. Common to many traditions is the story of two monks who see a woman drowning in a river. One dives into the water to save her, while the other looks on disapprovingly. When they return to the monastery, the latter accuses the former of breaking the monk's precept of touching a woman's body. His friend responds, "I let go of her on the bank of the river. You are still clinging to her."

Every ethical dilemma presents me with a uniquely complex situation that has never existed before and will never exist again. No number of precepts will ever be able to legislate for the infinite number of possible ethical dilemmas I may face. While precepts can take care of many simple choices, it is the dilemmas in life that cause me to agonize over them that demand the *practice* of ethics. For they call on me to look deeply at the situation and then choose, with wisdom, what to do. Such wisdom requires that I look beyond the wording of the precepts to the values they enshrine.

Action *(karma)*, declared the Buddha, is intention. To intend to do something is to choose to act in a certain way. Every such choice, however, is a risk; for I can never know the outcome of an action. All I can aspire to is the wisdom of knowing what might be best—a wisdom that requires the humility to acknowledge that I might get it wrong.

So the practice of ethics also entails the practice of meditation and wisdom. The Buddha's Threefold Training is present in any significant ethical act: as the commitment to a set of values embodied in precepts; as the clarity, stillness, and freedom of mindfulness that allows me to be aware of what is taking place at the moment; and as the wisdom to choose what might be the best thing to do.

In the Spring of 1993, I was fortunate to be part of a group of Western Buddhist teachers who met with His Holiness the Dalai Lama to discuss, among other things, Buddhist ethics, especially among teachers. The Dalai Lama is simultaneously a preeminent upholder of the historical Dharma and one of the foremost interpreters of its meaning. He is at once radically liberal in terms of doctrinal interpretation while highly conservative in matters of ethical orthodoxy.

It is the student, the Dalai Lama declares, who ultimately invests the teacher with authority by placing him or her in that role. Why is it that certain teachers in America and Europe have become embroiled in scandals? Why have they been able to exploit and abuse their students? This was an issue about which the Dalai Lama was deeply concerned.

The student, he noted, often fails to examine sufficiently the person's ethical and spiritual qualities before accepting him (it's usually "him") as a teacher. Yet the Tibetan tradition states clearly that one should devote years of close scrutiny before taking such a step. But the fault lies primarily with the teacher. The Dalai Lama observed, "Many friends I knew here [in India and Tibet] were very humble, but in the West they became proud." A simple monk catapulted from an impoverished settlement in India to a city in Europe and America to be revered and showered with wealth would understandably be prone to let such treatment go to his head. "Alcohol," His Holiness commented, "is often at the root of these problems." Of course: a tempting strategy for someone uprooted from his home-culture then thrust into a bewildering and demanding world for which he lacks the necessary social and emotional skills to cope.

That would be all very well except for the fact that most of these Asian teachers, and their Western successors, are supposed to be enlightened. What does "enlightenment" mean if those who have it are still subject to those less than edifying forms of behavior from whose grip we poor unenlightened souls are struggling to be free? At the very least, one would hope, enlightenment would imply a degree of contentment. But if someone were contented, why would he succumb to the conceit of self-importance? Why would he become dependent upon alcohol? Why would he indulge in a series of transient sexual encounters? Even unenlightened, contented people have no need for these things.

If a teacher's actions are unethical, responded the Dalai Lama, then even if they have practiced for many years, their practice has been wrong. Quite simply, they lack a proper understanding of the Dharma. There is a "gap" between the Dharma and their lives. He challenged the idea that once one has insight into the ultimate truth of emptiness, then one is no longer bound by the norms of morality. On the contrary: through revealing the web of relationships that ethically connects all living beings, the understanding of emptiness does not mystically transcend morality but grounds it in experience.

His Holiness expressed some concern that, on occasion, the Zen experience of *satori* is confused with either a deep state of concentration (samadhi) or simply a state of nonconceptuality, neither of which in themselves imply transformative understanding. The emphasis in Zen of high levels of enlightenment, he noted, might well entail the danger of leaving lower levels of simple neurotic behavior untouched. He likewise wondered about Buddhists he had met who talked of experiencing emptiness but seemed to lack human warmth, which indicated to him either a meditative lapse into sheer non-conceptuality or mental "sinking" (a subtle form of dullness). "Therefore," he concluded, "I prefer the gradual path."

Someone remarked that our days together "had a bone-deep sense of rightness" about them. The meeting with the Dalai Lama served as a confirmation of something many of us had intuitively known to be true all along, but had found neither the courage nor the words to express. "Past is past," said the Dalai Lama on the last day. "What is important? The future. We are the creators. The future is in our hands. Even if we fail, no regrets—we have to make the effort."

The Road Is Your Footsteps

Joan Halifax

Wanderer, the road is your
footsteps, nothing else;
wanderer, there is no path,
you lay down a path in walking.
In walking, you lay down a path

and when turning around
you see the road you'll
never step on again.
Wanderer, path there is none,
only tracks on the ocean foam. *

Whenever I think about keeping the precepts in the practice of Buddhism, I think about two qualities: discernment
and kindness. Can all of the precepts be categories of discernment and kindness, I ask myself. In one way, I think
they can. Or at least I wish they could be, as we practice
them in our daily lives. When I have read the Buddhist vows
of good and right conduct created since the time of
Gautama, many of the vows are tied to history and culture.
Yet when the precepts are brought up to date, when they
are made culturally relevant, as in the case of the Fourteen
Precepts of the Tiep Hien Order, or Thich Nhat Hanh's
retranslation of the Five Wonderful Precepts, our Buddhist

---

* "The Road Is Your Footsteps," by Antonio Machado, translated by Francisco
Varela.

vows are basically good medicine for our wayward minds and forgetful hearts. They remind us to see and point us toward kindness. Although our Original Nature might well be without blemish, most of us seem to have no small accumulation of "dust" on the mirror of our minds. Practice is about housecleaning. Precepts are a reminder that the house needs to be cleaned, and we best not forget that we forget to take care of ourselves and others. "Here's how," say the precepts.

Practice is as well about crafting the art of living beautifully, honestly, and with strength and dignity. Precepts are a refinement of this craft; they are a mindfulness tool and a tool of compassion that can open body, speech, and mind to original wholesomeness. Precepts are also about deepening the experience of community. Thây has said often that the precepts are our protectors: they protect us and they protect other beings as well. If we are to live in peace with each other, with the four worlds of Grandmother Earth, we dedicate ourselves to the path of nonviolence toward all. We see ourselves in each thing, in each being. We know that harming others through body, speech, or mind is harming a part of ourselves. We see that our so-called individual identity is tied to all other identities, and so we are not a separate or local self, but in a continuum with all else. Thus the precepts can bring us to this sense of deep responsibility toward the greater world and also responsibility for ourselves as well. They are, in essence, a way for us to take care of our global and very local community.

Yet the precepts also have their shadow. They can breed piety, self-righteousness, humorlessness, and even vengeance, behind what may be justified as "helpful criticism."

I have seen the precepts used as a weapon against others instead of as a tool of understanding. The humiliation and punishment of those who break the precepts seems to me to be counter to a Buddhist view of seeing ourselves as not separate from others and as empty of any indentity. There are saner means for creating understanding in those who are deluded or in the thrall of aggression or passion. The way to understanding is through understanding, to paraphrase Thich Nhat Hanh. How can we help a heart to undefend itself? I ask. How can our Original Innocence be retrieved? Certainly not through the coercion of punishment and public humiliation. This has been a big and sticky question in the Western Sangha. I believe we have not yet seen our way through to a solution of compassion for all. Suffering has many faces. Victim and tyrant both suffer. Alienation takes many forms, including greed, jealousy, sexual obsession, righteousness, anger, hatred, hypocrisy, and other forms of acute confusion. Suffering's face is abuser and abused.

It is also too often true that people hide behind the precepts and practice in secret the opposite of what they preach. Yet the fact is that we break precepts all the time. If we are able to see this, then there is some small possibility that we may cultivate compassion not only for our very human selves but for others as well. The Japanese have an expression that seems to capture the sense of pathos that is at the heart of our all too human dilemma: *mono no aware,* "the slender sadness." Simply by living we take life. Leather shoes and belts, breathing in and out, a cup of water, a flushing toilet, a stroll in the forest, raising mustard greens, flying here and there, the daily newspaper: in each, a thousand things are dying and being born. Our thoughts can never be as pure as white snow in a silver bowl. Our speech is only so skillful. Treating our bodies and the bodies of others as precious stuff is not so easy, driven as we are by duty or desire, fear or confusion. We are called to be honest about the struggle most of us face daily in living a wholesome life. Our world is not in a very healthy state. Between the degradation of our environment, the loss of values and meaning on a global and local level and the plain stuff of human suffering, the odds are pretty much against one realizing much long-lasting joy or equanimity. And this is why we practice: enlightenment is an accident; practice makes one accident-prone.

I believe that it is through our failures that the muscles of truth, compassion, and courage strengthen. Where we have been weak is where we find strategies for the development of our strengths. And often it takes a thorn to remove a thorn. Sometimes an act of so-called non-virtue is a helpful and skillful means. Striving for an unrealistic and exaggerated perfection is a madness that produces inauthenticity; in effect it can forge a monster of pretentiousness. Fall down into the darkness. Where are the knees of humility touching? Practice standing up. The spines of ten thousand things rise up with you. We are not alone in this wonderful struggle for truth. Thây once wrote that it is through our lives that we experiment with truth. The precepts are not truth. They usually point to the kindest alternative. But when a monk or nun in Vietnam offers the living body to the fire, where stands the truth of non-harming?

Once in the highlands of Nepal at Thupten Chöling Monastery near Junbese in the Solu Valley, hundreds of monks and nuns sat patiently in the *gompa* courtyard as the doctor with us gave them medical attention. Many were suffering from tuberculosis and cancer. All were smiling; self-pity was not present. We Westerners could hardly bear the sight of so much pain experienced with such great equanimity. When standing in their midst, I remembered the image of the first Vietnamese monk who immolated himself. His body in flames, he sat still in his own inferno, a "lotus in a sea of fire." Was it the precepts that brought him to this radical act of self-annihilation? In part, I believe that the precepts protected him as he gave his flesh to the flames. In taking his own life, he knew he might save many. And it takes keen and radical discernment as well as great love to make such an offering to others. Breaking the precepts, he kept the precepts.

What then can we do with the precepts? How can we live through them in a non-dual manner? What must be done to retrieve Original Innocence, our natural virtue? I believe it is not by putting something on that is not who we are. Wearing feathers does not make us a flying bird. The poet Antonio Machado reminds us that we lay down the road in the walking. The Buddha as he died told his friends that they were to question teachers and teachings. Take nothing on faith. Study the self, said Dogen. Cultivate discernment. Where one's foot is is where truth is to be found. Can we look deeply and see the universe in the dust beneath our feet? Penetrate the present moment sharply. And relax. "Use the precepts as a mirror," to quote Thich Nhat Hanh. Let the precepts be our ally, not our master. And know that the great question for most of us still remains unanswered.

The Practice of the Precepts
Richard Baker

Vowing is a fundamental practice in Buddhism because we are always vowing. Thinking and naming are implicit vows that things are as we think and the thing is as named. Language itself implicitly assumes — vows — that the world is permanent. Of course the world can be lived in for most practical purposes as if it were permanent; but it is not a wise way to live.

These tacit forms of vowing are habitual and often mistaken, so we need conscious, wise vows to counteract them. Views are vows that we take for granted. The Eightfold Path begins with Right Views, because views are the basis of all our activity and thinking. In Buddhist practice the first step in illuminating our views is taking the precepts. I call the precepts the vows of basic humanity because they are about what it is to be a human being. They describe what all societies hope human beings are like.

The sense of the practice of the precepts is found in the English word "precept": pre (before), cept (hold). Precepts are what we bring into the present, what we hold to be true, necessary, and responsible. The precepts should be a common sense that allows us to be at ease with ourself and responsibly present with others and the world. So a precept is what we hold, or could hold, before each moment begins. Thus as precepts can establish the conditions for how we think and act, they should be succinct enough to be implicitly present before we think and act. When they are, we will continuously discover and deepen our understanding of the precepts and of life itself, through our ordinary activity.

Karma is the baggage we accumulate. Dharma is functioning so that we put the baggage down and stop accumulating more. Precepts are the views that allow Dharma to function and thus are the foundation of Dharma practice and of the transformation of our life into Buddha's life.

Precepts can begin with studying ourselves from four points of view. First, there are our inner-requests, our secret desires for how we wish we and the world could be. Second, there are our outer precepts that we have from upbringing and experience. Third, there are the practical precepts that help us live in the world of our particular culture and time: norms that it makes sense to follow out of consideration for others and for our own well-being — as long as they are not damaging to ourselves or others.

Fourth, is taking and practicing the Buddhist precepts knowing that they are an expression of our basic humanity, and as well, the basis for realizing enlightenment and an expression of enlightenment. Most simply the Buddhist precepts are to recognize the impermanence, preciousness, and mystery of life; to do no harm; and to act to end suffering.

Ideally, through studying ourselves, other people, our culture, and the world, we will come to precepts that we can follow that are practical, that perfect our personality, that support others, and that protect life on this planet. Through many centuries and cultures, Buddhism has brought this study together in the expression of ten precepts.

Do not kill.
Do not take what is not given.
Do not be sexually irresponsible.
Do not lie.
Do not use or sell intoxicants in any way that harms or deludes.
Do not slander others.
Do not praise oneself.
Do not be possessive of anything.
Do not harbor anger or ill will.
Do not betray the minds of Compassion, Wisdom and Joy.

These are mostly obvious and almost go without saying; but they need saying. They need vowing. It makes a big difference when we consciously commit ourselves to our basic humanity. We turn around at the basis of our being. It is an act of "seeing" our life and taking responsibility for it. Taking the precepts turns us into more humane beings and sometimes into Buddhas: as it is both a step on the path and act of realization — the first enlightenment experience.

Following the precepts will transform our personal life and allow us to act with confidence in every situation. Precepts are guidelines, that give us balance and protection in both ordinary and extraordinary situations. Precepts allow us to put our personal and spiritual life in order and to act in the world with wisdom and compassion.

While we develop our understanding of the precepts in the many seemingly inconsequential details of life, the breaking of a precept is consequential. Breaking our own, inner precepts makes us sick or even crazy sometimes. Going against our culture's precepts and norms can be somewhere between discomforting and disastrous. And even though Buddhist precepts are guidelines and not cosmic laws, they are profoundly human principles and breaking them increases our karma, puts us out of balance, makes us sick, or worse.

We will understand the great applications and subtle nuances of the precepts when we hold them in view in our activity. For example, "not to kill," means to respect the interdependence of all sentient and insentient life. It also means to be aware that we are always killing something. Even if we are a vegetarian, the farmer clearing a field is killing insects and rodents. If we speak unkindly, we are killing something in ourself and in someone else. We suffer with any killing, even when it is unavoidable. Although these precepts are expressed minimally with: "do not," their practice is also "to do." In this precept, to practice whatever increases and supports life.

"Do not take what is not given" means do not have a greedy state of mind—and it also means to practice generosity. It means that all is our shared gift. If we walk into a room without thinking, we are taking that room before it is given. In practicing this precept, we might pause for a moment before each situation and action to allow it to be given to us.

"Do not be sexually irresponsible" means that sexuality should be mutual, and that it should not be addictive or harm anyone.

"Do not lie" means to recognize that life is based on the truth. It means that we should be completely truthful in thought, speech, and action. And it means the courage to be truthful about our faults. More subtly, if we do not feel nourished by our speech or actions then probably in some way we are speaking or acting falsely or harmfully and this would be to break the precept to not lie. In general when our behavior, our livelihood, or our states of mind are not nourishing, we are probably out of tune with the precepts.

"Do not use or sell intoxicants" means do not change your state of mind or another person's by some external means. If we change our state of mind, we do it through ourselves. Do not "sell" means that we are responsible for the actions that we cause in others. Suzuki-roshi said, "Do not present even Buddhism in an intoxicating way."

We should also be realistic about precepts. While they may turn us into more humane beings and even Buddhas, they do not turn us into presidents, lawyers, scientists, or artists. Precepts would undoubtedly make us a better president, and probably a better and more responsible scientist. But we still need training and sophistication to do the work of the world and to hope to solve its problems. Neither the precepts nor even the realization of enlightenment, equip us automatically for all the complexities of life—especially those we often face in contemporary society.

We may be willing to assume responsibility in our society, but the responsibility must be there to assume. Nowadays, situations can develop so quickly, at so many levels, that it is impossible for us to grasp historically, experientially, or intuitively their evolving dynamics in ways that allow fully understood responsible action. There are no simple answers to the ecological, political, economic, and spiritual problems that face us today. But armed with the precepts and with compassion and courage, we must try. The precepts are the starting point, as they are the foundation for developing practical wisdom and effective compassion.

When the precepts are held in view and realized in our activity, they bring a wholeness to our life and to our thoughts, speech and actions. The keeping or not-keeping of the precepts is reflected in all our states of mind and body. Keeping the precepts does not mean that we correct ourselves all the time. When we have come to a deep resolution through the precepts about how to live with ourselves, others, and the world, we develop states of mind that spontaneously express the precepts.

We practice the precepts by following them, by keeping them in view, and—through that—producing a precept-keeping state of mind. Instead of saying only, "How do we keep the precepts?" we can also ask, "What state of mind keeps the precepts?" When the precepts are present as thoroughly held intentions, they generate precept-keeping states of mind.

Every time we follow a precept we raise up the mind and consciousness of that precept. This affects every aspect of any situation. When informed by the precepts, our actions penetrate the immediate present and into the future.

When Buddha held up a flower before Mahakashyapa, he held up the mind of the precepts. And when Mahakashyapa smiled, he was following the precepts.

This flower-raising consciousness is always ready to be picked up—any situation will do. And smile-arising consciousness is always waiting to be smiled. We don't have to go back into the past, we don't have to wait for the Buddha to raise the flower, we can raise it ourselves. And we don't have to wait for Mahakashyapa to smile.

Taking the precepts protects us and develops our society. They are the seeds of our entire spiritual development. They are the mind of our Dharma ancestors. We are that flower that Buddha held up. We are Mahakashyapa's smile. It is said that when someone takes the precepts, flowers fall from the sky and the Earth trembles.

Commonly Asked Questions
Chân Không

Here are a number of responses we have offered to those who love the beauty and goodness of the mindfulness trainings, but hesitate to receive them formally:

Question: I was born a Christian. Do I have to abandon my faith to receive the Five Mindfulness Trainings formally?

Response: A tree that has no root cannot survive; you cannot grow well spiritually if you have no roots. You should not abandon your root religion. Please practice mindfulness as a base with the Five Mindfulness Trainings as guidelines. With mindfulness you can look deeply into your root tradition and discover many wonderful jewels in it. You might rediscover guidelines within your own tradition that you can share with both Christian and non-Christian friends.

Question: When I took the Five Mindfulness Trainings with another Buddhist teacher, the wording was not stated as clearly as it is in the mindfulness trainings of Thich Nhat Hanh. Can I take them again?

Response: Yes. The Five Mindfulness Trainings are from the Buddha. Your root teacher continues to be your root teacher. The new wording of the Five Mindfulness Trainings offered by Thây is to help you practice the teachings of the Buddha well. Your root teacher will be pleased if you renew your vows in this way. He or she will always be your first teacher. Thây Nhat Hanh will be your second, or third, or fourth teacher. We can have many teachers to enrich ourselves.

Question: I want to practice the Five Mindfulness Trainings, but why is it necessary to take refuge in the Three Jewels?

Response: Without a strong belief in these three precious jewels, you really cannot practice the Five Mindfulness Trainings. "I take refuge in the Buddha" means that I strongly believe in my ability to become enlightened, to transform my difficulties and be free of all suffering, and to be a source of joy and peace for myself and others. "Buddha" means the buddha in me, the potential for awakening in me. I know that Shakyamuni Buddha is my teacher. I also know that he is not a god.

"I take refuge in the Dharma" means that I believe in the practice of mindfulness, which brings understanding and love. I believe in the method that Shakyamuni Buddha offered from his own experience to me, so that I can realize the path that leads to freedom from suffering.

"I take refuge in the Sangha" means that I believe in the collective wisdom of a group of friends who vow to practice the same method as I do on our path of liberation. We need each other for support and to share our experiences of practice so that our perceptions will grow closer to reality and our actions will become more harmonious. We support each other on the path of realization, and in doing so collectively, our efforts benefit ourselves and all beings.

Without faith and confidence in the Three Jewels, it is difficult to practice the Five Mindfulness Trainings well.

Question: Can I take only one, two, three, or four of the Five Mindfulness Trainings?

Response: The Buddha said yes, you can. If you practice even one mindfulness training deeply, you will find that you are also keeping the other four, even without making a formal promise to do so. The Five Mindfulness Trainings are very much interconnected.

Question: If I take the First Mindfulness Training, does it mean I have to become a vegetarian?

Response: Thây Nhat Hanh asks us to practice mindfulness deeply every time we eat or drink. If we do so, we may find that our appetite for meat and fish begins to diminish. The important thing is to be aware of what we consume. I have met people who cannot be vegetarian because of medical reasons, but who respect life more than many vegetarians. Some vegetarians are too extreme, and are unkind to those who cannot give up meat-eating. I am more comfortable with a meat-eater than an extremist vegetarian who is filled with self-righteousness.

Question: Many of my friends, including myself, have two or three sexual partners. How do you suggest that I keep the Third Mindfulness Training?

Response: When you do two or three things at the same time, like eating your dinner, watching television, and having a conversation with friends at the dinner table, you do

not do any of the three things deeply. You cannot truly taste
and enjoy each morsel of food that your beloved one prepared for you. You cannot give your full attention to the
television program, and you will be unable to listen carefully
to what your friends are saying. It is even more difficult if
you have several sexual partners at the same time. Please
examine this deeply. None of your relations will be profound. Ask your heart whether you are really happy. It may
seem all right now, but are you certain that you are not
causing suffering to yourself or your partners? A superficial, noncommitted relationship never leads to real happiness or peace.

Question (from a teenager): In my school, everyone my age
is sexually active. Why shouldn't I be? If I don't act like
them, my friends will think I'm odd.

Response: A sexual relationship is a very deep act for mutual peace and the preservation of the species. Acting in a
superficial way damages our body and mind. When our
mind is not ready for such a deep act, our feelings, perceptions, and understanding towards that friend will not be profound enough, and a sexual act will increase the risk of
destroying the friendship. You may think that a sexual act
is just like any other act you do for fun or enjoyment, but
many young people have told me that they realize afterwards that it was a mistake. Sex is deeper than other acts.
The hurt from having sex in a noncommitted way can be
profound, and the wound may remain unhealed for many
years. Birth control has nothing to do with these mental
wounds. Many teenagers report that they had no joy in their

life, no desire to live after receiving a mental wound from having a sexual relationship they were not ready for. Usually we only share our very deep secrets with those with whom we have had a long experience of appreciation and trust. This is also true with our bodies. We shouldn't share our bodies with someone with whom we do not intend to have a long-term commitment.

Question: Can I take the Fifth Mindfulness Training, and still drink an occasional glass of wine or beer with dinner?

Response: Thây Nhat Hanh advises us not to drink any alcohol, if possible. If you still have a strong inclination to drink, please do so mindfully. Look deeply into the conditions of your liver, your heart, and the fact that humankind is wasting a lot of grain and fruit making alcohol instead of feeding other humans. Meditating in this way will lead us to feeling uncomfortable when drinking any amount of alcohol.

If you are not ready to stop drinking entirely, please take the first four mindfulness trainings and try to drink mindfully until you are ready to stop. Thây Nhat Hanh advises those who take the Fifth Mindfulness Training not to drink at all, even one glass of wine or beer a week. French authorities advise their citizens that one glass of alcohol is okay, but that three is saying hello to the damage that an accident can cause. But how can you have a second or third glass if you haven't had the first?

Under normal conditions, we may drink one or two glasses of wine from time to time. But in moments of despair, we might have five, six, or seven glasses in order to forget our sorrows. This can lead to alcohol abuse. A lovely grand-mother on a retreat in England asked this question, and I told her, "You are a moderate drinker, but are you sure all your sons, daughters, and grandchildren are like you? If during one or two moments of despair they gradually drink more and more and become alcoholic and destroy them-selves physically and mentally, who would be responsible? Haven't you participated partly in that process? If you keep the Fifth Mindfulness Training now, you may be the torch for the future generations of your grandchildren. You keep the mindfulness trainings as a bodhisattva and not as an order that you are forced to obey.

Question: If I break a training, to whom should I confess?
Response: Confess to your own Buddha. The best way to practice is with a group of friends, even just one or two. Making efforts to follow this path of beauty, you can share with them your successes and failures. Reciting the mind-fulness trainings regularly, with the group, helps very much. During the Mindfulness Trainings recitation, following the reading of each training, this question is asked, "Have you made an effort to study and practice it during the past two weeks?" If you have broken the training, you can say, si-lently, to yourself, "I am deeply aware that I was not mindful and have broken this mindfulness training. From now on, I will try to do better." Don't feel too guilty. Your habit energy is still strong. The fact that you are aware of your negative act will decrease that habit energy each time you recite the training, and soon your habit will be transformed.

Question: In tending a garden, I often find it necessary to kill certain "pests"—worms, insects, and rodents that destroy the garden. Is this against the First Mindfulness Training? Also, I don't know how to deal with infestations of ants, cockroaches, and other household "pests." How does a practicing Buddhist deal with these problems?

Response: Even when we boil a kettle of water, we must be aware that we are killing many microorganisms in the process. Our effort is not to kill, so we try various methods to do the least harm to all living creatures. For example, in gardening, we learn about how to grow certain plants next to our cultivated flowers and vegetables that repel insects, worms, and rodents. We try our best not to use harmful pesticides, but use organic ones that don't kill the animals if possible. Likewise, we try to keep out ants and cockroaches by harmless means—keeping food out of their reach, using organic repellents, or just being patient. If finally, we deem it necessary to kill these creatures, it is most important to be aware of the fact that we are indeed killing them. With mindfulness, we continue to make efforts not to do harm (even as we are aware that harm has been done). Nonviolence can never be absolute. But we can continue to do our best to minimize the harm we cause and to maximize our appreciation and reverence for all life—people, animals, plants, and minerals.

I would like to tell you about a friend named James, who has suffered tremendously. As a child of five, he was beaten by his mother and pushed down two flights of stairs on his bicycle. He recalled how all the acts of violence from his mother followed a period when she was drinking. One day, he was beaten until his left eye was badly swollen and blue. At school, when his teacher asked why his eye was swollen, he told the truth. His teacher called home, and his mother denied that she had beaten her son. At forty-two, James still cries like a five-year-old when he recalls, "He believed her, and I was punished for lying. I continued to tell the truth, and they punished me."

His mother sent him to live with his grandmother, who used drugs and alcohol. When he was seven, she began to abuse him sexually and beat him, especially when she was drunk. Other unbelievable acts of violence were inflicted on him as a result of her use of drugs or alcohol. He ran away from his grandmother's home and went back to his mother, but she too began abusing him sexually. So finally he saved enough money to escape to his father. When he called him to say he was in town and wished to live with him, his father panicked and sent him back home.

When he was seventeen, his father encouraged him to join the army and go to Vietnam. Before he said good-bye, his father gave him a slap on the back and said, "The army will make a man out of you, son." James cried again.

One afternoon, in Plum Village, James described how overwhelmed with despair he was looking at all the young Vietnamese boys and girls, who reminded him of those he had killed in Vietnam. After several days and nights of gunfire from his helicopter, he would get out of his plane and discover human bodies stacked on each other like logs in rows for several hundred meters. "How could I bring these bodies back to life?" His friends tried to comfort him, saying, "That's what war is, James, you couldn't help it." James can tell you how, looking back over his life, the roots of war began in the violence of his parents' divorce and his parents' alcoholism and sexual abuse.

I have been an assistant of Thây Nhat Hanh in leading many retreats on mindfulness practice for Vietnamese and Western friends since 1983. I always encourage people to tell their difficulties to Thây, so he can help them transform their long-lasting pain. But as Thây cannot see everyone, I have listened to many people's pain. The story of James is one of dozens of similar stories from war veterans and others. So many had fathers or mothers who were alcoholics, and so many came from broken families. At first, I thought this was an American problem, but later, while assisting Thây on retreats in England, Germany, Switzerland, Italy, and France, I heard the same sad stories there. So much suffering comes from the fact that people drink too much, are irresponsible with their sexual conduct, lie, cause suffering to others with their unmindful speech, or spread news they are not sure is true. So many people were raised by drunken adults, or adults with polluted minds who abused children, because the adults themselves had been victims during their own childhoods. I realized that adults who terrorize their children were themselves victims.

A way out of the suffering is for us to join with a group of people who are joyful and who try to practice going in the direction of goodness, beauty, and truth. The people in the group must sincerely look at their own weaknesses, smile at them, and consider the weaknesses as part of the compost to be transformed into flowers.

Today there are so many polluted minds and such an atmosphere of violence and abuse. We need to find a way out. The Five Mindfulness Trainings represent a beautiful road that leads to awakening. Even if we ourselves were not abused as children or have no problems with alcohol abuse, sexual irresponsibility, etc., we can help many others by formally receiving these trainings and practicing them. We can be an example for many people, and help lead them in the direction of joy and peace.

To practice the Five Mindfulness Trainings, it is helpful to remember these points:

— Mindfulness is the ground of all the trainings. We would not need to keep any particular training if we were capable of being mindful twenty-four hours a day. But since that is not the case, we need to practice the Five Mindfulness Trainings or their equivalent as a guideline.

— The wording of the Five Mindfulness Trainings presented by Thây Nhat Hanh in this book is in the spirit offered by Shakyamuni Buddha, updated to respond to the needs and difficulties of people of our day.

— No one can keep the mindfulness trainings totally. Even the Buddha himself could not do this. When boiling vegetables to eat, we kill microorganisms in the water, or when taking an antibiotic, we kill microorganisms in our intestines. If we live mindfully, it is good enough to gently move in the direction of acting without violence.

— The direction of the Five Mindfulness Trainings is the direction of beauty, goodness, and truth. To transform our collective consciousness into beauty, goodness, and truth, we move in that direction, as we would go in the direction of the sun. We cannot climb onto the sun, and we don't need to. To move in that direction is good enough.

— As we try our best to move in that direction, knowing that no one is able to live up to his or her best, we need a group of friends with whom we can practice regularly and share our experiences of living the mindfulness trainings. As we encounter difficulties, Thây Nhat Hanh says, we must practice with a Sangha and regularly recite the trainings together to remind and inspire each other and try to find ways out of the most difficult situations in our families and society. That is why Thây says that the ordination ceremony will be nullified if the ordinee does not recite the mindfulness trainings at least once every three months with his or her Sangha.

As Patricia Marx Ellsberg points out in her essay, the situation of the world today is so violent and confused that for a future to be possible, not only individuals, but even nations need to take the Five Mindfulness Trainings.

PART THREE

The Three Jewels

The Three Jewels
Buddha, Dharma, Sangha

I take refuge in the Buddha,
the one who shows me the way in this life.

I take refuge in the Dharma,
the way of understanding and love.

I take refuge in the Sangha,
the community that lives in harmony and awareness.

In the Buddhist tradition, whenever you vow to study, practice, and observe the Five Mindfulness Trainings, you also take refuge in the Three Jewels. To practice the Five Mindfulness Trainings is to have faith in the path of mindfulness, understanding, and compassion, because the Five Mindfulness Trainings are made of these three elements. The Three Jewels are made of the same elements. Mindfulness, understanding, and compassion are universal values that transcend cultural boundaries. In every spiritual tradition, there is the equivalent to the Five Mindfulness Trainings and the Three Jewels.

When we were in our mother's womb, we felt secure — protected from heat, cold, hunger, and other adversities. Although we were not yet aware in the way we are now, we knew somehow that this was a safe place. The moment we were born and came into contact with adversity, we began to cry, and since that time we have yearned for the security of our mother's womb.

We live in a world that is impermanent and filled with suffering, and we feel insecure. We desire permanence, but everything is changing. We desire an absolute identity, but there are no permanent entities, not even the one we call our "self." To seek for refuge means, first of all, to look for a place that is safe, secure, and permanent, something we can rely on for a long time. We want a place like Heaven, where a strong, stable figure, like God the Father will protect us, and we will not have to worry about anything. But Heaven is in the future.

In Asian literature, some poets expressed the belief that they lived in a safe, happy place before being exiled to Earth, and when they died, they would be able to return to that state of bliss and happiness. Other Asians believed that they were gods in previous lives but, because of mistakes they made, they were exiled on Earth. If they performed meritorious deeds in this life, they believed they would be able to return to that safe place. The wish to take refuge is a universal desire to return to a place where we are safe and secure. In Vietnamese, the words for "to take refuge" are literally, "to go back and rely on."

But how can we feel safe now? Things *are* impermanent. If a kernel of corn is not impermanent, it will never grow into an ear of corn. If your daughter is not impermanent, she will never grow up into a beautiful, young lady. If dictatorships are not impermanent, there is no hope of replacing them. We need impermanence and we should be happy to

say, "Long live impermanence, so that life can be possible."
Still, in the depths of our being, we yearn for permanence.

In Buddhism there are two kinds of practice—devotional
and transformational. To practice devotion is to rely primarily on the power of another, who may be a buddha or a god.
To practice transformation is to rely more on yourself and
the path you are following. To be devoted to the Dharma
is different from practicing the Dharma. When you say, "I
take refuge in the Dharma," you may be showing your faith
in it, but that is not the same as practicing the Dharma. To
say "I want to become a doctor" is an expression of the determination to practice medicine. But to become a doctor,
you have to spend seven or eight years studying and practicing medicine. When you say, "I take refuge in the Buddha, the Dharma, and the Sangha," this may be only the
willingness to practice. It is not because you make this statement that you are already practicing. You enter the path of
transformation when you begin to practice the things you
pronounce.

But pronouncing words does have an effect. When you
say, "I am determined to study medicine," that already has
an impact on your life, even before you apply to medical
school. You want to do it, and because of your willingness
and desire, you will find a way to go to school. When you
say, "I take refuge in the Dharma," you are expressing
confidence in the Dharma. You see the Dharma as something wholesome, and you want to orient yourself toward
it. That is devotion. When you study and apply the Dharma
in your daily life, that is transformational practice. In every

religion, there is the distinction between devotional practice and transformational practice.

Many Buddhists recite the Three Refuges as a devotional practice. We need faith and confidence in order to practice. In Buddhism, faith and confidence are linked to each other, and sometimes mean the same thing. However, blind faith is not encouraged. We have to see, touch, experiment with, and verify things before we truly believe in them. The Buddha, the Dharma, and the Sangha are things we can touch. They are not matters of speculation. The Buddha is a human being who lived in history. His life and teachings are known to us. We can use our time, energy, and intelligence to get in touch with the Buddha. Real faith and confidence arise from being in touch, not just from someone saying something we are expected to believe.

We can go directly to the Dharma. The Dharma exists in written form, in the tradition, and in the practice of people. Where people are practicing the Dharma, we can see the fruit of their practice. The Dharma is also something concrete that we can touch, experiment with, and verify, and this brings about real faith and confidence.

The Sangha is a community that practices the Dharma. A good Sangha expresses the Dharma. When we see a practicing Sangha that reveals some degree of peace, calm, happiness, and transformation, faith and confidence arise in us. Imagine I am someone who has not had anything to believe in for a long time. I have had no peace. But suddenly I see a community of people who have transformed themselves to some extent through the practice. Now I have faith and confidence, and that brings me some degree of peace. Devotion in Buddhism is not accepting a theory without touching the reality.

Many laypeople in Buddhist countries recite, "I take refuge in the Buddha, I take refuge in the Dharma, I take refuge in the Sangha," but they rely on monks and nuns to practice for them. They support the practicing Sangha by offering food, shelter, and other things that help the Sangha succeed in its practice of the Dharma. They feel that the practice of one person living in real happiness brings happiness to many people. This is devotional practice. For these people, to pronounce the words, "I take refuge in the Buddha, I take refuge in the Dharma, I take refuge in the Sangha" is already enough to have peace and joy. But in North America and Europe, laypeople want to practice transformation. The vipassana meditation community in the West, for example, is comprised of people who practice—they do not just rely on monks and nuns—and there are many lay teachers.

When the layman Anathapindika was about to die, the Venerable Sariputra, knowing how much Anathapindika loved the Buddha and had faith in the Dharma and Sangha, invited him to meditate on the Three Jewels. Anathapindika felt great relief and was then invited by Sariputra to meditate on other subjects usually reserved for monks and nuns. These experiences watered Anathapindika's seeds of peace and joy.

A few months before he passed away, the Buddha taught his disciples to take refuge in themselves. "Bhikkhus, be an island unto yourself. Don't take refuge in anything else. Take refuge in the Dharma. Use the Dharma as your lamp.

Use the Dharma as your island." He prepared very well for his passing away.

The Buddha said, "My physical body will not be here, but my Dharma body *(Dharmakaya)* will be with you forever. If you want to take refuge in my Dharma body, you can do that at any time." In later Buddhist history, the Dharma body became the spirit or the soul of the Buddha, i.e. the true Buddha that is available throughout time. If we know how to touch the Dharmakaya, it is available to us, our children, and their children at anytime. To see clearly that the physical body is not as important as the Dharma body was a comfort to the Buddha's disciples. Today our society has so much suffering and danger in it, like a strong current trying to pull us into the ocean of sorrow. To protect ourselves, we too can practice being islands unto ourselves.

Sanghakaya is a new word. Every Buddha and every practitioner has his or her Sangha body. A Buddha can only be a Buddha when the Dharma is in him or her. Without the Dharma, someone cannot be called a Buddha. The Buddha and the Dharma are two, but one. A Buddha cannot be without the Dharma. The Dharma cannot be without the Buddha. A Sangha is a community that practices the Dharma. If there is no Sangha, who is practicing the Dharma? The Dharma is not tangible if there are no practitioners. If you want the Dharma to be practiced, you need a Sangha. Therefore the Sangha contains the Buddha and the Dharma. The Buddha, the Dharma, and the Sangha inter-are. They might be called the Buddhist Trinity: *triratna* (or *ratna traya*), the Three Jewels. In the triratna, each jewel contains the other two. When you take refuge in one, you take refuge in all three. When you have confidence and trust in the Sangha and practice with the Sangha, you are expressing your confidence in the Buddha and the Dharma. It is crucial to practice the mindfulness trainings with a Sangha, a community of practice. You need a Sangha to support you in the practice. A true Sangha always possesses in its heart the Buddha and the Dharma.

Devotional practice in Buddhism is based on what can be seen, heard, and touched. If we are not in touch with the physical Buddha, we cannot be in touch with the Dharma body of the Buddha, or the Sangha body of the Buddha. Because we have information about the life of the physical Buddha, our devotion is well-grounded. This is also true in Christianity. Jesus is someone we can touch. Information about his life and teachings is available.

In the *Anguttara Nikaya,* the Buddha said that when you are agitated, afraid, lacking in confidence, or weak, if you practice taking refuge in the Buddha, the Dharma, and the Sangha, your fear and instability will dissolve. He told the story of the fighting between Sakra, the king of the gods, and the *asuras*. Sakra commanded his troop of *devas*, or heavenly soldiers, to fly his flag of seven jewels. Every time they lacked confidence in fighting the asuras, if they looked at the flag, they would find the strength and confidence needed. This is natural. If you have confidence in your commander, you will fight well as a soldier. When you believe in a good cause, you have the courage to stand your ground. The Buddha used this example to talk about taking refuge. When you have doubts, weakness, or agitation, if you focus your attention on the Buddha, the Dharma, and the

Sangha, you become firm again. This is the fruit of practicing the Three Refuges in its devotional form.

But taking refuge can also be a transformational practice. What makes the Buddha a Buddha is enlightenment, the living Dharma, which is the fruit of practice. The *Tripitaka,* the three baskets of the teachings, is the Dharma, but not the living Dharma. The Dharma as audio tapes, video tapes, or books is not the living Dharma. The living Dharma must be observed in a Fully Enlightened One, a Buddha, or in those not yet fully enlightened who are really practicing. The essence of the Dharma is enlightenment, which is to understand, to be aware.

The practice of mindfulness is the key to enlightenment. When you become aware of something, you begin to have enlightenment. When you drink a cup of water and are aware that you are drinking a cup of water deeply with your whole being, enlightenment in its initial form is there. To be enlightened is to be enlightened on something. I am enlightened on the fact that I am drinking a cup of water. I can get joy, peace, and happiness just because of that enlightenment. When you look at the blue sky and are aware of the blue sky, the blue sky becomes real, and you become real. That is enlightenment, and enlightenment brings about true life and true happiness.

The substance of a Buddha is mindfulness. Every time you go back to your breath and practice breathing deeply in mindfulness, you are a living Buddha. When you are not sure what to do, go back to your breath—breathe in and out consciously—and take refuge in mindfulness. The best thing to do in moments of difficulty is to go back to yourself and dwell in mindfulness. When you are in bed and unable to sleep, the best thing to do is go back to your breathing. You are safe and happy knowing that no matter what happens, you are doing the best thing you can do. Taking refuge in the Buddha, not as a devotion, but as true practice, is very comforting. Every time you feel confused, angry, lost, agitated, or afraid, you always have a place which you can return to. Mindfulness of breathing is your own island. It is very safe. "Be an island unto yourself" means that you should know how to go back to yourself in case of danger, instability, or loss. This practice of taking refuge is very concrete. When you go back to your breath —breathing in and out deeply—and light the lamp of mindfulness in yourself, you are safe. In that state of mindfulness, you are truly yourself. The lamp is already lit, and the possibility of seeing things more clearly is great.

Suppose you are on a boat crossing the ocean. If you get caught in a storm, stay calm and don't panic. To accomplish that, you go back to your breathing and be yourself. Because you are calm, truly your own island, you will know what to do and what not to do. If you do not, the boat may capsize. We destroy ourselves by doing things we ought not do. Take refuge in mindfulness, and you will see things more clearly and know what to do to improve the situation. This is a very deep practice. Mindfulness brings about concentration, and concentration brings about insight and wisdom. This is the safest place to take refuge now, and not just in the future.

The safety and stability that your island can provide depend on your practice. Everything—baking a cake, building a house, playing volleyball—depends on your practice. If you are a beginner who practices going back to your island of self every time you feel upset, you will enjoy some mindfulness, concentration, and peace. The moment you begin to practice, Buddha, Dharma, and Sangha are available to you to some extent. But this cannot be compared to the mindfulness, concentration, and peace of someone who has been practicing for a long time. At first, your Buddha may be just some information you have read about him, the Dharma just what you have heard from a friend, and the Sangha a community you have touched once or twice. As you continue to practice, the Buddha, the Dharma, and the Sangha will reveal themselves more fully to you. Your Buddha is not identical to my Buddha. They are both Buddha, but the degree to which that is revealed depends on our practice.

The Buddha taught that there are three fundamental characteristics of life: impermanence, no-self, and nirvana. A teaching that contradicts any of these Three Seals is not an authentic Buddhist teaching. If we don't know that everything is impermanent, we will suffer. If we don't know that everything is without a self, without an absolute identity, we will suffer. But there is the possibility of not suffering, thanks to nirvana. Nirvana is the absence of delusion concerning the nature of impermanence and selflessness. When you look deeply into the true nature of reality, if you realize the nature of impermanence and no-self, you are free from suffering. You may think that nirvana is the opposite of impermanence and no-self. But if you continue to practice, you will see that nirvana is found in the world of impermanence and no-self.

Visualize the ocean with countless waves on it. On the one hand, we see that all waves begin with birth and end with death. They can be big or small, high or low. If we look into their nature, we see that the waves are impermanent and without a self. But if we look more deeply, we see that the waves are also water. The moment the wave realizes that it is water, all fear of death, impermanence, and non-self will disappear. Water is, at the same time, wave and not-wave, yet waves are made only of water. Notions like big or small, high or low, beginning or end, can be applied to waves, but water is free of all these distinctions. Nirvana can be found in the heart of life which is characterized by birth and death. That is why, if you practice taking refuge deeply, one day you will know that you are free from birth and death. You are free from the kinds of dangers that have been assaulting you. When you are able to see that, you will be able to construct a boat to ride on the waves of birth and death, smiling, like a bodhisattva. You will no longer fear birth and death. You do not have to abandon this world and seek some faraway paradise in order to be free.

The Buddha rarely talked about nirvana, the unconditioned, because he knew that if he talked about it, we would spend all of our time talking about it and not practicing. But he did make a few rare statements concerning nirvana. Let us read this statement from *Udana* VIII, 3: "Verily, there is an unborn, unoriginated, uncreated, unformed. If there were not this unborn, unoriginated, uncreated, unformed, then an escape from the world of the born, the originated, the created, and the formed, would not be possible." Early Buddhism did not have the ontological flavor we see in later Buddhism. The Buddha dealt more with the phenomenal world. His teaching was very practical. Theologians spend a lot of ink, time, and breath talking about God. This is exactly what the Buddha did not want his disciples to do, because he wanted them to have time to practice *samatha* (stopping, calming), vipassana (looking deeply), taking refuge in the Three Jewels, the Five Mindfulness Trainings, and so on.

In other places, the teaching of the Buddha reveals to us the unconditioned. For instance, he says, "When conditions are sufficient, the eyes are perceived by us as existing. When conditions are no longer sufficient, the eyes are not perceived by us as existing. The eyes have not come from somewhere in space. The eyes will not go anywhere in space." The idea of coming, going, being, and nonbeing are representations and concepts to be extinguished. If there is something that you cannot talk about, it is best not to talk about it. Wittgenstein said the same thing in his *Tractatus Logicos-Philosophicus:* "Concerning that which cannot be talked about, we should not say anything." We cannot talk about it, but we can experience it. We can experience the non-born, non-dying, non-beginning, non-ending, because it is reality itself. The way to experience it is to abandon our habit of perceiving everything through concepts and representations. Theologians have spent thousands of years talking about God as one representation. This is called onto-theology, and it is talking about what we should not talk about.

The Buddha that we experience here and now is mindfulness. Mindfulness is a mental formation like any other mental formation. It has a seed in our individual consciousness and in our collective consciousness. It is a precious gem buried deep in the Earth for us to discover and explore. When we unearth it, we can transform the whole situation. This is the coming of a Buddha — not from nothingness, not from nonbeing, but from a Buddha seed, Buddha nature. The Buddha nature is, first of all, mindfulness. The practice of mindfulness is the practice of bringing the Buddha into life in the present moment. It is the real Buddha. That is why the Buddha is sometimes described in Mahayana Buddhism as the *Tathagata* ("he or she who has come from suchness, from reality-as-it-is"). Suchness cannot be described with words or concepts. Nirvana, the absolute truth, reality-as-it-is, is the object of our true perception and insight. But an object of perception always includes the subject of perception. With mindfulness, we can see the nature of reality clearly. Mindfulness, with the support of concentration, conscious breathing, and looking deeply, becomes a power that can penetrate deeply and directly into the heart of things. It is not speculation, using concepts and words, but direct looking. Finally, the true nature of reality will be revealed to us as suchness. Reality-as-it-is cannot be described by words and concepts, but can be penetrated by prajña, true understanding. In each of us, the seed of mindfulness can be described as the womb of the Buddha (*tathagatagarbha*).

We are all mothers of the Buddha, because all of us are pregnant with a Buddha. If we know how to take care of our baby Buddha, one day this Buddha will be revealed to us. That is why at Plum Village we bow to each other as a sign of greeting, saying silently, "A lotus for you, a Buddha to be." We see the other person as the mother of a future Buddha. In each of us is a Buddha-embryo, the seed of mindfulness, and this is what we need to take refuge in in our daily lives. The Buddha is said to have ten names, and the first, Tathagata, means "one who has arrived from suchness, remains in suchness, and will return to suchness." Like the Buddha, we have come from suchness, remain in suchness, and will return to suchness. We have nowhere to go, have come from nowhere, and are going nowhere.

It is not just absolute reality that cannot be talked about. It is not just the Buddha who is like that. We are also like that. Nothing can be conceived or talked about. A glass of orange juice itself is absolute reality. We cannot talk about orange juice to someone who has not tasted it. No matter what we say, the other person will not have the true experience of orange juice. The only way is to drink it. It is like a turtle telling a fish about life on dry land. You cannot describe dry land to a fish. He could never understand how one might be able to breathe without water. Things cannot be described by concepts and words. They can only be encountered by direct experience.

When Wittgenstein said, "That which cannot be talked about should not be talked about," you might think there are things that we can talk about and things we cannot. But in fact, nothing can be talked about, perceived, or described by representation. If you talk about things you have not experienced, you are wasting your time and other people's time as well. As you continue the practice of taking refuge, you will see this more and more clearly, and you will save a lot of time, paper, and publishing enterprises, and have more time to enjoy your tea and live your daily life in mindfulness.

The second name of the Buddha is *Arhat,* meaning "one who is worthy of our support and respect." The third is *Samyaksambuddha,* "one whose knowledge and practice are perfect." The fourth is *Vidyacaranasampana,* "one who is equipped with knowledge and practice." The fifth is *Sugata,* "one who is welcome." The sixth is *Lokavida,* "one who knows the world well." The seventh is *Anutta-rapurusa-damyasarathi,* meaning "unsurpassed leader of people to be trained and taught." The eighth is *Sastadeva-manussana,* "teacher of gods and humans." The ninth is Buddha, "enlightened one." The tenth is *Bhagavat,* "blessed one." Every time we take refuge in the Buddha, we take refuge in the one who has these attributes. When we take refuge in our mindfulness, we take refuge in the seed of these attributes in us.

In Mahayana Buddhism, the womb of the Tathagata, tathagatagarbha, is equivalent to the Dharmakaya, body of the Dharma. When we talk about suchness or nirvana, we are talking about that which should not be talked about. The Buddha mostly refrained from talking about these things, but he did, from time to time, offer a hint by talking about other things. The teaching of no coming, no going, no being, no nonbeing was already very clear in early Buddhism. In Mahayana Buddhism, these ideas became fully developed, sometimes a little overdeveloped. We should not indulge ourselves too much in things like that. We should preserve the practical nature of the Buddhadharma. Otherwise we will become philosophers and not practitioners.

When I practice taking refuge in my breathing, I say, "Breathing in, I go back to myself. Breathing out, I take refuge in my own island. Mindfulness is the Buddha that illuminates my path." I practice mindful breathing as a practice of taking refuge.

We live in a world of impermanence and non-self, a world in which many waves are trying to carry us away. We practice dwelling in our mindfulness as our own island. Mindfulness is the Buddha in person. It is also the Dharma and the Sangha. Practicing mindful breathing, we shine the light of mindfulness upon the five *skandhas*, or aggregates of being, namely, form, feelings, perceptions, mental formations, and consciousness in us. There is a Sangha of five elements inside us, and there may be a lack of harmony among them. Suffering results from conflicts between skandhas. Mindfulness of breathing can calm the conflicts and reestablish harmony in us. The fruits of this practice are peace and joy.

When you look deeply, the nature of non-birth, non-death, non-coming, non-going are revealed to you, and the fear that you may lose this or that will disappear. You do not have to abandon this world. You do not have to go to heaven for refuge. You do not have to wait for the future to have refuge. You take refuge here and now. The depth of your refuge depends on your practice. Buddha, Dharma, and Sangha are always available. The womb of the Tathagata is always there. We only need to go back there in order to be safe.

In the Greek Orthodox church, theologians talk about *"apophatic* theology," or "negative theology." "Apophatic" is from the Greek word *"apophasis,"* which means "denying." You say that God is not this, God is not that, until you get rid of all your concepts of God. The second century Buddhist philosopher Nagarjuna developed a similar dialectic to remove our ideas concerning reality. He did not describe reality, because reality is what it is and cannot be described. When Zen Buddhists talk about killing the Buddha, they mean that the Buddha-concept should be killed in order for the real Buddha to be directly experienced.

The idea of the Trinity in the Orthodox Christian church is quite deep and sophisticated. Sometimes our friends in the Orthodox church say that the Trinity is their social program. They begin with the Holy Spirit and the Son. The Father may be more difficult to touch, think about, or perceive. The Father belongs to the realm of inexpressibility and should be kept in that mystical realm. But it is possible to touch the Son and the Holy Spirit. Similarly, in Buddhism we talk about practicing with the Dharma and Sangha, and later on, touching nirvana, "the Tathagata-womb."

The Holy Spirit creates the Son, so the Son can show us the way to the Father. I told a Christian monk, "It is much safer to begin with the Holy Spirit. You have the capacity to recognize the presence of the Holy Spirit whenever and wherever It manifests Itself. It is the presence of mindfulness, understanding, and love, the energy that animates not only Jesus but all of us. That energy helps us recognize the Living Christ and touch the ground of being that is God the Father. In Buddhism, the Holy Spirit is called mindfulness, awakening, prajña, maitri, and karuna. Touching this energy, you touch the Buddha and nirvana."

The theology of the death of God, the idea of atheistic and secular Christianity is very much in the same spirit. You depend on the person of Jesus Christ and his teaching and practice. This is very intelligent and pragmatic. If you begin with the idea of God, you may get stuck. In the Greek Orthodox church, the idea of deification, that a person is a microcosm of God, is very inspiring. It was already evident in the fourth century, and it is very much like the Asian tradition that states that "the body of a human being is a mini-cosmos." God has made humans so that humans can become God. A human being is a mini-God, a micro-theos. This is close to the idea that the Tathagata is in every one of us. We are all pregnant with a Buddha. According to the theology of deification, humans are made in order to participate in the divinity of God, not just as separate creations. Deification is made not only of the spirit, but of the body of a human also. According to the teaching of the Trinity in the Orthodox church, the Father is the source of divinity who engenders the Son. With the "Word" (Greek: *logos*), he brings about the spirit that is alive in the Son. This is comparable to the non-dual nature of the Buddha, Dharma, and Sangha.

The most important thing in a multi-religious dialogue is for each side to tell the other side how they practice. If we come together for five or ten days, we should be able to share with each other how we live our daily lives, how we practice taking refuge, how we pray, meditate, and so on. To me the Five Mindfulness Trainings are the practice of mindfulness. The Three Refuges are also the practice of mindfulness. "I take refuge in the Sangha" is very much a practice, and not a devotion.

Mystery in Christianity sometimes is described as darkness. By the third or fourth century in the Greek Orthodox church, the idea of darkness was already there, and it has become a source for Christian mysticism. Darkness means that you cannot know it; you cannot see it clearly with your intellect; it is mysterious. When Victor Hugo lost his daughter Leopoldine, he complained that "Man sees only one side of things, the other side is plunged into the night of the frightening mystery." In Buddhism, mystery is described in terms of light. In the *Avatamsaka Sutra,* the Buddha is light. If you are struck by one of the beams, you will get enlightened. In the *Avatamsaka Sutra,* the Buddha was giving a talk in the form of Vairocana Buddha, that is, the Dharmakaya Buddha, and humans, gods, Buddhas, bodhisattvas, carpenters, kings, policemen — everyone in the assembly experienced bliss because they had been touched by the beams of light emanating from the Buddha. In Buddhism, the word *"avidya"* means the lack of wisdom, insight, and light. *Vidya,* understanding, is made of light. Everything that is mystical and wonderful is on the side of the light, not on the side of the darkness. Although it cannot be grasped by conceptual knowledge, it is light.

In a short story, Alphonse Daudet talks about a shepherd on a mountain who made the Sign of the Cross when he saw a shooting star. The popular belief is that at the moment you see a shooting star, one soul is entering heaven. Making the Sign of the Cross is a form of taking refuge in the Trinity:

the Father, Son, and the Holy Spirit. When you believe that something is the embodiment of evil, you hold out a cross to chase it away. In popular Buddhism, when people see something they think of as unwholesome, they also invoke the name of Buddha. That is a practice of devotion. When there is light, darkness disappears.

But if we learn the principle of non-duality, our understanding changes. One practice of mindfulness is to recite this verse as we turn on the light in a room:

> Forgetfulness is the darkness,
> mindfulness is the light.
> I am bringing in mindfulness,
> to shine upon all life.

We may understand this as a kind of fight between light and darkness, but in reality, it is an embrace. Mindfulness, if practiced continuously, will be strong enough to embrace your fear or anger and transform them. Reciting a mantra is not like holding out a cross to chase away evil. It should be practiced in a nonviolent, non-dualistic way.

In Christianity, taking refuge is expressed by the body of Jesus. To some people, the image of the cross expresses too much suffering. There must be ways to represent the Father, Son, and Holy Spirit as peace, joy, and happiness other than through the image of the cross. Some people say that they feel more peaceful when they see the image of the Buddha sitting and smiling. To look at a person being crucified for two thousand years may be too much. I like very much that the practice be manifested in a body, but what about an image of Jesus holding a lamb? That may be more appealing. When we practice sitting meditation, it is expressed in the body. When we practice prostrations, it is also an act of taking refuge. All the five elements are all focused in one direction, the pole of mindfulness.

In Christianity, the Eucharist is an act of taking refuge in Jesus, God. Not much is said about experiencing deeply the Dharma and the Sangha. Without the Sangha, the community in the church, and without the eating of bread and drinking of wine in awareness, there could be no Jesus. The Sangha has been important in Christianity. People never celebrate a Eucharist on their own but come together as a Sangha. In the early church, the expression "we are all one body" was much used. But the hierarchy of the church became oppressive and the Sangha weakened as a result.

In Buddhist practice, we stress the Sangha. If you leave the Sangha, it is said to be like the tiger leaving his mountain. A tiger that comes to the lowlands can be caught by humans and killed. A practitioner without a Sangha can lose his practice.

Sangha means community. There are four communities — monks, nuns, laymen, and laywomen. I add the supportive elements that are not human, like trees, cushions, rocks, water, and birds. A pebble, a leaf, a dahlia, a tree, a bird, and a path, are all preaching the *Saddharmapundarika Sutra,* if we know how to listen. In the *Pure Land (Sukhavativyuha) Sutra,* it is said that when the wind blows through the trees, we can hear the teaching of the Four Establishments of Mindfulness, the Eightfold Path, the Four Powers, and so on. The whole cosmos is preaching and practicing the

Buddhadharma. If we are attentive, we can touch that Sangha.

Everyone who wants to practice needs a Sangha. We have to set up small Sanghas around us to support us in the practice. Without a Sangha, when we become exhausted, we will have no means to nourish ourselves. By creating a small Sangha, you can find the greater Sangha around and inside us.

The practice of taking refuge can be done every day, several times a day. Every time you feel unwell, agitated, sad, afraid, or worried—these are times to go back to your island of mindfulness. If you practice going back to your island when you are not experiencing difficulty, when you do have a problem, it will be easier and more enjoyable. Do not wait until you are hit by a wave in order to go back to your island. Practice going back to your island by living mindfully every moment of your life. If the practice becomes a habit, when the difficult moments arrive, it will be natural and easy to do. Walking, breathing, sitting, eating in silence, and drinking tea in mindfulness are all practices of taking refuge. Every mindfulness practice contains all the other practices. If you just practice taking refuge, you are also practicing the Eightfold Path, the Four Establishments of Mindfulness, and everything else. One Dharma door contains all Dharma doors.

Taking refuge is not a matter of belief. It is very grounded in our experience. You know that you have the seed of mindfulness in you. You have the island within yourself. It is not a metaphysical question. Your in-breath and out-breath are available; your seed of mindfulness is always there. Taking refuge is a matter of daily practice. In Buddhist temples, we use the words *"công phu"* (Chinese: *kung fu*), which mean "daily practice," not "martial arts." A good student or teacher always goes back and takes refuge in the mindfulness of breathing when he or she is angry or worried.

When we receive bad news and we feel shaken by it, the best thing to do at that moment is to take refuge. In the West, when you have to tell someone bad news, you ask him to sit down. Sitting down is good, because you are afraid he will faint. But you can also ask him to breathe in and out to be calm and solid. Even good news can make someone faint. If you hear that you have just won ten million dollars in the lottery, you might have a heart attack and die.

It is not always easy to practice taking refuge in this way. Because of our tendency to believe in a permanent self, we need to practice deeply enough to realize the nature of no coming, no going. Otherwise, we will stick to the idea that before we were born, we were somewhere, and when we die, we go somewhere. Because we don't know where we are going, we feel afraid. The teaching of the Pure Land assures people that if they practice well now, they will be reborn in the Pure Land of Amida Buddha. There are other Pure Lands as well, such as the Abhirati of Aksobhya. Many Buddhists want to be reborn in Tushita Heaven to be with the Buddha Maitreya, and when the time comes for him to be reborn on Earth, they want to come with him. To be reborn in the Pure Land, you have to practice recollection of the Buddha *(buddharusmrti)*. During your daily life, you invoke the name of the Buddha and focus your attention on the Buddha. This is a form of taking refuge. You practice either by visualizing the Buddha, with his thirty-two beautiful marks, or by invoking his name. The name of the Buddha can bring about the good qualities of the Buddha. During the time you practice, you dwell in that kind of refuge of the Buddha. You are close to him, to the island. You water the seed of Buddhahood—mindfulness and goodness—in yourself. Later you learn from your teacher that the Pure Land is in your heart. These are gradual steps toward the teaching of no coming and no going. Many people need a place to go before they realize that they do not have to go anywhere.

We have to remember that Pure Lands are impermanent. In Christianity, the Kingdom of God is the place you will go for eternity. But in Buddhism, the Pure Land is a kind of university where you will practice with a teacher for a while, graduate, and then come back here again. An enlightened being named Amida Buddha asked those who have an affinity with the practice to come with him and practice, so that they can graduate one day and become fully enlightened persons. If you realize that the Pure Land is in your heart, as in the teaching of the *Avatamsaka Sutra,* you don't need a faraway place or time to set up a Pure Land. You can set up a Sangha, a mini-Pure Land, right now at home.

I would like to rephrase the classic formulas for taking refuge: "Going back, taking refuge in the Buddha *in myself,* I vow to realize the Great Way in order to give rise to the highest mind." The highest mind is *bodhicitta,* the intention or vow to practice and help countless living beings until you attain full enlightenment. There are those who practice just to relieve their own suffering and don't think about the suffering of others. That is not the highest mind.

"Going back, taking refuge in the Dharma *in myself,* I vow to attain understanding and wisdom as immense as the ocean." The living Dharma can be touched only through the manifestation of a Buddha, a Sangha, or a good practitioner.

"Going back, taking refuge in the Sangha *in myself,* I vow, together with all beings, to help build a Sangha without obstacles." If you are motivated by the desire to set up a small Sangha in order to practice and to make friends happy with the practice, you are practicing the Third Refuge. If you suffer because you do not have confidence in your practice and feel on the verge of leaving the Sangha, that is unfortunate. If you feel unhappy in the Sangha, if you find your Sangha too difficult to handle, it is best to make the effort to continue. We do not need a perfect Sangha. An imperfect one is good enough. We can do our best to transform ourselves into a positive element of the Sangha and encourage the rest of the group to be supported by our effort.

The Three Refuges are a very deep practice. We have simplified the phrasing into these simple words so that even young people can understand easily:

I take refuge in the Buddha,
the one who shows me the way in this life.

I take refuge in the Dharma,
the way of understanding and love.

I take refuge in the Sangha,
the community that lives in harmony and awareness.

We know that the Three Jewels inter-are. Without a Dharma and a Sangha, a Buddha is not a Buddha. Even Buddhas-to-be need a Dharma body and a Sangha body. These are up to us to build. Our Dharma body should be a living body and not just a set of dogmas or ideas. Our Sangha body should be a living community, and not just a dream of looking for land or looking for like-minded people. The best way is to manifest it here and now, to make this Sangha a living Sangha today, to make the Dharma that we have learned the living Dharma today. If we are determined, everything will come together. Learning from the *Sutra on Knowing the Better Way to Live Alone,* we practice in the present moment to enjoy the present moment, which is our Sangha here and now.

A Buddha like Shakyamuni can be seen through his Dharma body and his Sangha body. When you touch his Dharma body or his Sangha body, you touch him. We should not complain that we were born 2,500 years too late and therefore cannot touch him. We *are* touching him. We are touching his Dharma body and his Sangha body right now. All of us Buddhas-to-be need to express ourselves in our Dharma body and in our Sangha body. When someone says something that provokes us, we can smile and return to our breathing, and he or she will have a chance to touch our Dharma body. When we act mindfully and compassionately, our Dharma is the living Dharma. Every time we have some difficulty or frustration, if we go back to our breathing and dwell in our island of mindfulness, everyone can touch our living Dharma. When we have a group of friends who support each other in the practice of the Dharma, every time someone joins us for a cup of tea, they touch our Sangha body.

The Buddha said that his body of teachings would remain with his students, but that it was up to them to make it last. If we don't practice, there will be only books and tapes, but if we practice, the Dharma body will be a living Dharma. "Dharmakaya" later acquired the meaning "soul of the Buddha," "spirit of the Buddha," "true Buddha," "ground of the Buddha." It developed an ontological flavor, "ground of all beings," "ground of all enlightenment." Finally, it became something equivalent to "suchness," "nirvana," and "tathagatagarbha" ("the womb of the Tathagata"). That is a natural development. The Dharma is the door that opens to all of these meanings. We only need to be concerned about how much time we spend talking about these things.

Dharmakaya is the Buddha in substance. Sometimes we call it *Vairocana,* the ontological Buddha, the Buddha as the base, the embodiment of the Dharma, always shining, always enlightening trees, grass, birds, human beings, and so on, always emitting light. It is that Buddha who is preaching the *Avatamsaka Sutra* now and not just 2,500 years ago. Those who get in touch with Vairocana do not need Shakyamuni. Shakyamuni is just a beam of rays sent by Vairocana Buddha. Shakyamuni is the Nirmanakaya, the transformation body, a spark sent forth by the center of the fire, a beam sent by the sun. We don't need to worry if one beam ceases to be apparent. The sun is always there. The Dharmakaya is always there. If you cannot listen directly to Shakyamuni, if you are open enough, you can listen to Vairocana. In addition to Shakyamuni, many transformation Buddhas are preaching. The trees, birds, violet bamboos, and yellow chrysanthemums are all preaching the same Dharma that Shakyamuni taught 2,500 years ago. We can be in touch with the Nirmanakaya, through either.

The first body is the *Dharmakaya*, the second body is the *Sambhogakaya*, and the third body is the *Nirmanakaya*. The Sambhogakaya is the body of bliss. You can get in touch with that body because the Buddha fulfilled his wish of full enlightenment. Mindfulness is the base of understanding, compassion, peace, and happiness. When we breathe in and out and become aware of the blue sky, we enjoy it. When we take our tea in mindfulness, we are in touch. Peace, joy, and happiness are the fruits of mindfulness. The Buddha who practices mindfulness has immeasurable peace, joy, and happiness, and we can touch this body of enjoyment. Every time you touch something in harmony, something that shines, you touch the Sambhogakaya of the Buddha. That is the rewards body, the body of enjoyment, symbolizing the peace and happiness of the Buddha, the fruit of his practice.

The rewards body can be described in two ways. The first is self-enjoyment. The second is the enjoyment experienced by others. When you practice mindfulness, you enjoy within you the fruit of the practice. Those around you also enjoy your happiness and the fruits of your practice. When someone is happy and peaceful, that happiness and peace radiates around him or her for others to enjoy. If you practice well, you will be able to send many Sambhogakayas into the world in order to help relieve the suffering of living beings. One person has the capacity of transforming many living

beings if she knows how to explore the seed of enlightenment within her.

One day when I was in an airplane, I had this thought:
If the pilot were to announce that the plane was about to
crash, what would I do? It was clear to me that I would
practice mindful breathing, and smiling. That is the best
thing I could do in that moment. And if, down there, you
knew that I was practicing breathing and smiling during
that difficult moment, you would have confidence in yourself. It is essential that we do not wait until such a critical
moment in order to begin the practice.

I always practice mindful breathing during takeoffs and
landings. That does not mean that in between I do not do
this, but I never fail to do it at these times. It is not because
I'm afraid, but it has become a habit. I travel so much. I also
have the habit of practicing walking meditation at airports.
I always try to leave for the airport early, so that I will not
have to rush when I am there. Everyone is rushing, but I
know it is possible to be yourself and practice walking meditation even there.

The Three Jewels and the Five Mindfulness Trainings
are both teachings about the practice of mindfulness. The
Three Jewels embrace every teaching and are the foundation of every practice. This is the kind of practice you can
gauge. You will be able to see the progress you are making.
Your trust and faith in the Three Jewels will be strength-
ened every day.

It may sound as though devotion practice and transformation practice are completely distinct but that is not correct. Both are active practices. Devotion practice can also

be transformational. Devotion practice relies more on the other, although there is also self-effort. Transformation practice is to rely on what is in yourself, but since you need a Sangha and a teacher, you also count on the other. The distinction is not absolute, but there is a distinction.

Mindfulness practice can be found in both devotional and transformational practice. Many people think that mindfulness practice is the only Buddhist practice. Mindful breathing unites body and mind. That is the first condition to touch anything you want to touch, even a higher being. When you practice mindful breathing, you become peaceful and solid, and your being is already higher.

PART FOUR

The Sutra on the White-Clad Disciple

The Sutra on the White-Clad Disciple
(Upasaka Sutra, no. 128 of the Madhyama Agama)

I heard these words of the Buddha one time when he was staying at the monastery in the Jeta Grove near Sravasti that had been donated by the layman Anathapindika. On that day, Anathapindika came with five hundred other lay students of the Buddha to the hut where Sariputra resided. They all bowed their heads in reverence to Sariputra and sat down respectfully to one side. Venerable Sariputra offered them skillful teachings, bringing them joy and confidence in the Three Jewels and the practice of the true Dharma. Then, Sariputra and all five hundred laymen and women went together to the hut of the Buddha, where Sariputra, Anathapindika and the other five hundred laymen and women, prostrated at Buddha's feet and sat down to one side.

When he saw that everyone was seated, the Buddha addressed Sariputra, saying "Sariputra, if lay students of the Buddha, those who wear white robes, study and practice the Five Mindfulness Trainings and the Four Contemplations, they will realize without hardship the capacity to abide happily in the present moment. They know they will not fall into the realms of hell, hungry ghosts, animals, and other suffering paths.

Translated from Sanskrit into Chinese by Gotama Sanghadeva in the years 397-398. Translated from Chinese by Thich Nhat Hanh, in consultation with *Anguttara Nikaya* III, 211.

"Such men and women will have attained the fruit of stream-enterer and they will have no fear of descending into dark paths. They are on the way of right awakening. They will only need to return to the worlds of gods or men seven more times before attaining perfect liberation and the end of suffering.

"Sariputra, how do lay students of the Buddha, those who wear white robes, study and practice the Five Mindfulness Trainings and the Four Contemplations?

"Lay students of the Buddha move away from killing, put an end to killing, rid themselves of all weapons, learn humility before others, learn humility in themselves, practice love and compassion, and protect all living beings, even the smallest insects. They uproot from within themselves any intention to kill. In this way, lay students of the Buddha study and practice the first of the Five Mindfulness Trainings.

"Lay students of the Buddha move away from taking what has not been given, put an end to taking what has not been given. They find joy in being generous without expecting anything in return. Their minds are not obscured by greed and craving. They constantly guard their own honesty and uproot from within themselves any intention to take what has not been given. In this way, lay students of the Buddha study and practice the second of the Five Mindfulness Trainings.

"Lay students of the Buddha move away from sexual misconduct, put an end to sexual misconduct, and protect everyone—those under the care of their father, mother, or both father and mother; their elder sister or elder brother; their parents-in-law or other in-laws; those of the same sex; the wife, daughter, husband or son of another; and those who have been raped, assaulted, or tortured sexually, or who are prostitutes. Lay students of the Buddha uproot from within themselves any intention to commit sexual misconduct. In this way, lay students of the Buddha study and practice the third of the Five Mindfulness Trainings.

"Lay students of the Buddha move away from saying what is not true, put an end to saying what is not true. They say only what is true, and they find great joy in saying what is true. They always abide in truth and are completely reliable, never despising others. They have uprooted from within themselves any intention to say what is not true. In this way, lay students of the Buddha study and practice the fourth of the Five Mindfulness Trainings.

"Lay students of the Buddha move away from drinking alcohol, put an end to drinking alcohol. They uproot from within themselves the habit of drinking alcohol. In this way, lay students of the Buddha study and practice the fifth of the Five Mindfulness Trainings.

"Sariputra, how do lay students of the Buddha attain the Four Contemplations and abide happily in the present moment with ease and without hardship? They practice being aware of the Buddha, meditating on the one who has come from suchness and returns to suchness as one who is truly and fully awakened, without any attachments; as one whose understanding and practice are perfect; as the Well-Gone One; as one who knows and fully understands the world; as one who has attained the very highest; as one who has tamed what needs to be tamed; as a teacher of humans and gods; as an awakened one; and as a World-Honored One. When they meditate in this way, all unwholesome desires come to an end and impure, sorrowful, and anxious elements no longer arise in their hearts. As a result of contemplating the Buddha, their thoughts are clear, they feel joy, and they arrive at the first of the Four Contemplations, abiding happily in the present moment, with ease and without any hardship.

"Sariputra, the lay students of the Buddha practice being aware of the Dharma, meditating as follows: the Dharma is taught by the Lord Buddha with great skill; it can lead to complete liberation; it can lead to a state of no afflictions; there is not the pain of heat in it; its value is timeless. When lay students of the Buddha meditate on and observe the Dharma in this way, all unwholesome desires come to an end, and impure, sorrowful, and anxious elements no longer arise in their hearts. As a result of contemplating the Dharma, their thoughts are clear, they feel joy, and they arrive at the second of the Four Contemplations, abiding happily in the present moment, with ease and without any hardship.

"Sariputra, the lay students of the Buddha practice being aware of the Sangha, meditating as follows: the noble community of the Tathagata is advancing on the right direction, it is on the path of righteousness, it is oriented towards the Dharma, and lives the teachings in the way they are meant to be lived. In that community, there are the Four Pairs and the Eight Grades — realized Arhats and those who are realizing the fruit of Arhatship, non-returners and those who are realizing the fruit of non-returning, once-returners and those who are realizing the fruit of once-returning, and stream-enterers and those who are realizing the fruit of stream-entry. The noble community of the Tathagata has successfully realized the practice of the precepts *(sila)*, the practice of concentration *(samadhi)*, and the practice of insight *(prajña)*. It has liberation and liberated vision. It is worthy of respect, honor, service, and offerings. It is a beautiful field of merit in our lives. As a result of contemplating the Sangha, their thoughts are clear, they feel joy, and they arrive at the third of the Four Contemplations, abiding happily in the present moment, with ease and without any hardship.

"Sariputra, the lay students of the Buddha practice being mindful of the Mindfulness Trainings, meditating as follows: the Mindfulness Trainings have no drawbacks, no flaws, no impurities, and no unsound points; and they help us abide in the land of the Tathagata. The Mindfulness Trainings are not of the nature to deceive. They are always praised, accepted, practiced, and guarded by the holy ones. As a result of contemplating the Mindfulness Trainings, the students' thoughts are clear, they feel joy, and they arrive at the fourth of the Four Contemplations, abiding happily in the present moment, with ease and without any hardship.

"Sariputra, please remember that white-clad disciples of the Buddha who practice in this way will not descend into hell realms, hungry-ghost realms, animal realms, or any other realms of suffering. They have experienced the fruit of stream-entry, which means not falling into paths of hardship and wrongdoing. Having entered the stream, they cannot help but go in the direction of right awakening. They will only need to return to the world of gods or humans seven more times before they arrive at the frontiers of complete liberation and the ending of sorrow."

At that time the Lord, the World-Honored One, pronounced these verses:

An intelligent man or woman who lives a family life
and realizes how fearful the hell realms are,
is encouraged to receive and practice the right
teachings and put an end to paths of suffering.

She studies and learns to deepen the practice—
not killing living beings,
speaking of things as they really are,
and not taking what is not given.

He is faithful to his spouse,
moving away from the habit of sexual misconduct,
determined not to ingest
intoxicants,
keeping his mind frenzy-free.

She is always aware of the Buddha,
the Dharma, and the Sangha.
Contemplating the Mindfulness Trainings,
her mind arrives at peace, joy, and freedom.

If he wants to practice generosity
in order to cultivate the garden of happiness,
then his guideline is learning the path
of liberation and awakening.

Sariputra, listen carefully
with regard to this point:
Look carefully at the herd
of oxen over there.

Some oxen are white and yellow.
Some are black or red.
Some are brown with yellow spots,
while others are grey like pigeons.

Whatever their color
or place of origin,
their value to us lies
in their ability to transport.

Healthy and strong ones
who pull carts vigorously,
can make many journeys
and are the most useful.

In our human world,
there are Brahmans, warriors,
scholars, tradesmen,
and artisans.

But the truly virtuous men and women
are those who practice the Wonderful Mindfulness
Trainings and are able to realize liberation.
Like the Well-Gone One, they live in true freedom.

There is no need to discriminate
according to family or caste.
To realize the greatest happiness
is to make offerings to those who are truly virtuous.

A person who lacks in virtue
or is poor in insight
cannot light the way for others.
To make offerings to such a one
bears little fruit.

Sons and daughters of Buddha
who practice the way of insight
and have their minds directed to Buddha
have strong, stable roots
and are reborn only to be happy.

Returning to the worlds of gods and humans
no more than seven times,
they eventually realize nirvana,
transforming all their suffering
into joy and purity.

Thus spoke the Buddha. The Venerable Sariputra, the other monks and nuns, the layman Anathapindika, and the other five hundred laymen and laywomen heard these words and were delighted to put them into practice.

Commentaries on the Sutra

INTRODUCTION

Many people regard Buddhism as a religion, but if we say that it is a way of life, we may be closer to the truth. Life is the art of bringing happiness to ourselves and others. If we ourselves are not happy, we cannot make others happy, and if others are not happy, we cannot be truly happy either. To practice the art of bringing happiness to ourselves and others, we need to have faith and confidence in something that we find true and beautiful, that accords with the truth, and that can be a foundation for true and lasting happiness. Because we need such faith, Buddhism is also called a religion. Faith here does not mean faith in a creator god or a metaphysical first principle, the existence of which we cannot really prove. Faith here means confidence in something beautiful and true that can bring about happiness and that we can actually touch.

The *Sutra on the White-Clad Disciple* is one of the most basic discourses of the Buddha, and it is easy to understand and practice. Its theme is the cultivation of faith in a life of happiness. The Buddha was not addressing superhuman beings; he was talking to ordinary people like you and me. Anyone can put these teachings into practice and bring about their own happiness, the happiness of those they love, and the happiness of others, including animals, plants, and minerals, right in the present moment.

The *Sutra on the White-Clad Disciple* presents two basic practices for lay Buddhists—the Five Mindfulness Trainings *(pañca-sila)* and the Four Contemplations *(anusmrti)*. If we practice according to the instructions given in this sutra, we will live happily in the present moment *(dittha-dhamma sukha-vihari)*, certain that we will not be drawn into difficult and painful destinies *(durgati)*. Because the Five Mindfulness Trainings are the fruit of the practice of mindfulness, to practice these mindfulness trainings is to practice mindfulness and to guarantee our security, freedom, and happiness.

As the fruit of the practice of mindfulness, the Five Mindfulness Trainings contain within them the Three Jewels — Buddha, Dharma, and Sangha. Their essence is the insight and compassion of the Buddha himself. Buddha is not a god. Buddhahood, or Buddha nature, is the seed of love and understanding that is within each of us. Buddhists sometimes say that Buddha is mind. Dharma is the way of understanding and love practiced by the Buddha. And Sangha is the community of those who dwell together in harmony, practicing the Dharma, under the guidance of the Buddha. The practice of these mindfulness trainings is an expression of faith and trust in the Three Jewels, and gives us the protection of the Three Jewels. The Four Contemplations — the contemplations of Buddha, Dharma, Sangha, and the Mindfulness Trainings—are the same. They are practices that go along with the Five Mindfulness Trainings and help us see into the depths of the Five Mindfulness Trainings in order to discover and generate the energy of love and understanding, which is the essence of the mindfulness trainings.

THE TEXT

In the Chinese Major Buddhist Canon *(Tripitaka)*, this discourse is called the *Upaṣaka Sutra*. It is also entitled *The White-Clad Disciple*, or *The One Who Wears the White Robe*. It is sutra number 128 in the *Madhyama Agama*, which can also be found in *Taisho* number 26. It was translated from Sanskrit into Chinese by Gotama Sanghadeva in the Eastern Chin Dynasty at the end of the fourth century (397-398), and transmitted by the Sarvastivada school in Kashmir. In the *Pali Canon*, the corresponding sutra is called the *Householder Sutta* and is found in the *Anguttara Nikaya*, reference A III, 211. It was transmitted by the Tamrasatiya school and preserved in Sri Lanka. Tamrasatiya is the original name for the school we now call Theravada. The content of the *Householder Sutta* and the *Upaṣaka Sutra* is essentially identical. The manner of expression in the two discourses varies, but the principal ideas are the same.

The Sarvastivada and the Vibhajyavada schools of Buddhism came into existence in the third century B.C.E., during the reign of King Asoka. Of these two most important schools, one went to the north and one went to the south. The monks of the Sarvastivada school went to Kashmir in northwestern India, where their school flourished for more than one thousand years. It was here that the *Sutra Pitaka* was collated and the *Abhidharma Pitaka* of the Sarvastivadan school originated. Both were subsequently brought to China and translated into Chinese. Many branches derived from the Vibhajyavada school, including the Tamrasatiya, so-called because the monks wore bronze-colored robes. This school was brought to Sri Lanka in the time of King Asoka and continues there to this day. Mahinda, a son of King Asoka, had a part in the continuation of this transmission.

At that time, both schools relied on oral transmission for the sutras, the *vinaya* (monastic code) and the *abhidharma*. They were written down only in the first century B.C.E. Despite this, when we compare the two versions (the *Upasaka Sutra* and the *Householder Sutta*), we can see that the content of the two is essentially identical. This is something of a miracle. While translating the *Upasaka Sutra* and writing this commentary, I consulted the *Householder Sutta* and felt very grateful to have access to the two versions.

THE CIRCUMSTANCES UNDER WHICH THE SUTRA WAS DELIVERED

The Buddha gave these teachings at the Jeta Grove Monastery in Sravasti to an audience of laymen and laywomen headed by Anathapindika. Anathapindika always gave his whole heart to the service of the Buddha; the Dharma, the teachings of the Buddha; and the Sangha, the community of practitioners. It was he who purchased the grove that belonged to Prince Jeta outside of Sravasti so that he could offer it to the Buddha and his community of monks and nuns, and it was he who supported the community in making that beautiful park into a monastery. He was honored among the businessmen of Sravasti, the capital of the kingdom of Kosala, and was so well-known as a protector and sponsor of the poor that people of his time gave him the name *Anathapindika* (Sanskrit: *Anathapindada*), "he who supports the poor and the abandoned." His given name was Sudatta. His faith in the Three Jewels—Buddha, Dharma, and Sangha—was strong, and he and those close to him practiced according to the teachings of the Buddha. His consort Puññalakkhana also knew the practice. They had three daughters—Big Subhadha, Little Subhadha, and Sumagadha—followed by one son, Rula, and all four of them had confidence in the practice of the Buddha's teachings. Anathapindika's family was a very happy one.

As we might expect, the layman Anathapindika had many friends in business and intellectual circles, and he often brought these friends into contact with the Buddha and the Sangha. On the day the Buddha offered the *Sutra on the White-Clad Disciple*, Anathapindika brought his friends to the Jeta Grove Monastery to visit Sariputra and hear Sariputra give a Dharma talk. After Sariputra's talk, he and his friends went to see the Buddha, and it was in the presence of Sariputra that the Buddha taught this sutra. The sutra says that Anathapindika came that day with five hundred friends, but this number is just a symbolic way of saying a considerable number of people. This sutra lays the very foundation for lay practice. In both the Pali and Chinese versions of this sutra, laypeople are referred to as "those who are dressed in white." Those who did not wear white were the monks and nuns. Therefore the sutra is named the *Sutra on the White-Clad Disciple*.

The relationship between Sariputra and Anathapindika was a special one. Anathapindika first met the Buddha in the Bamboo Grove Monastery, near Rajagriha, the capital of Magadha. He loved and respected the Buddha and wished very much that the Buddha would come to his own country, Kosala, to teach the Way of Awakening. To his delight, the Buddha accepted his invitation. He allowed Sariputra to go to Sravasti with Anathapindika in order to make advance preparations for his visit and the teachings he would give. When the two of them came to Sravasti, Anathapindika introduced his family and friends to Sariputra and invited Sariputra to stay in the capital to give teachings while he searched for land to set up a future prac-tice place for the Buddha and the community of monks. He was able to buy a beautiful grove of trees from Prince Jeta, and this park became the Anathapindika Monastery. When, in the *Sutra on the White-Clad Disciple,* we see Anathapindika bringing five hundred friends to visit Sariputra, we are reminded of the deep friendship between Sariputra and Anathapindika, dating from the time they walked together from Magadha to Kosala. Some years later, when Anatha-pindika was near the end of his life, it was Sariputra who sat by his bed and taught him the meditation on looking deeply into birth and death, and this helped Anathapindika leave this life with a heart filled with peace and joy.

The Buddha taught this sutra for laypersons in the pres-ence of Anathapindika and his friends, but he addressed Sariputra. This is further evidence of the close relationship between Sariputra and Anathapindika.

The Chinese version of the sutra is entitled the *Upasaka Sutra.* Literally, *"upasaka"* means "someone who is near." In this context, it means someone who is close to monks and nuns in order to learn and to practice. The feminine form is *upasika.* There is a Mahayana sutra entitled the *Upasaka Sila Sutra (Taisho* 1488), in which the Three Jewels and the Five Mindfulness Trainings are explained in the Mahayana spirit. This sutra is a development of the *Sigalavadana Sutra* (*Taisho* 16). It talks about giving rise to *bodhicitta,* the aspiration to help all beings attain enlightenment, observing the mindfulness trainings, and practicing meditative concentration and insight with energy, and is related to the bodhisattva mindfulness trainings in the *Mahayana Brahmajala Sutra* (*Taisho* 1484). We should not confuse the *Upasaka (White-Clad Disciple) Sutra* with the *Upasaka Sila Sutra.*

THE CONTENT OF THE SUTRA

The *Sutra on the White-Clad Disciple* establishes the foundation for the lay practice of Buddhism and clearly states the objects of a lay Buddhist's faith and confidence that lead to the path of happiness and liberation for oneself and others. In the sutra, the Buddha taught that lay students who steadily practice the Five Mindfulness Trainings and the Four Contemplations—of the Buddha, the Dharma, the Sangha, and the Mindfulness Trainings—have the capacity to live joyfully and at peace right in the present moment and attain the fruit of stream-enterer (*srotapanna*), which means they will never again fall into hell, hungry-ghost, or animal realms.

THE FIVE MINDFULNESS TRAININGS

In order to practice the Five Mindfulness Trainings, we need to have confidence in their efficacy. Mindfulness trainings describe a way to live that brings peace, joy, and happiness. We can have faith and confidence in the mindfulness trainings as the embodiment of that which is true, wholesome, and beautiful. Mindfulness trainings show us the way in this life. They protect us, our family, and our society, and can be seen as the foundation of happiness for the family and society. Because they prevent us from falling into the abyss of wrong views and wrong actions, mindfulness trainings are the object of our faith and confidence. Faith here is not blind faith or some groundless belief. It is the kind of faith that is based on experience. When we study and practice the mindfulness trainings, our understanding of them grows deeper day by day.

Thanks to the study and practice of the Five Mindfulness Trainings, we can see how necessary they are for us, our families, and our society. They are as necessary as sunlight for plants, and oxygen for us. The Five Mindfulness Trainings are a fruit of the Buddha's experience and also the experience of many generations who have practiced them. Living in mindfulness, we can see that if we do not practice the Five Mindfulness Trainings, we, our families, and our society will be on the path of suffering and degeneration. The Five Mindfulness Trainings are not only the art of living; they are also the basis of our faith and confidence. The Buddha taught that if we know how to practice the Five Mindfulness Training-Dharmas, we will know how to be happy in the present moment.

The First Mindfulness Trainings — Not to Kill

"Lay students of the Buddha move away from killing, put an end to killing, rid themselves of all weapons, learn humility before others, learn humility in themselves, practice love and compassion, and protect all living beings, even the smallest insects. They uproot from within themselves any intention to kill."

The First Mindfulness Training expresses the principle of protecting life — not just the lives of human beings but of all species, even the smallest of beings.

Our practice here is not limited by the outer form. The teaching of the Buddha is clear: "They uproot from within themselves any intention to kill." This mindfulness training is first of all a mindfulness training for our mind. We can protect life with our bodies and our words, but to observe this mindfulness training is, above all, to protect life with our minds. If we want to uproot the intention to kill, we need to practice the Four Great Intentions Minds: humility before others, humility in ourselves, compassion, and loving kindness. Humility before others (Sanskrit: *apatrapa*) is to see our own weaknesses in comparison with others and to see how others are able to protect life in ways we cannot yet do. Humility in ourselves (Sanskrit: *hri*) is to know our own shortcomings when we hurt another living being or are not able to protect the life of another living being. Loving kindness (Sanskrit: *maitri*) is to offer joy to someone. Joy is the fruit of living in peace, not threatened by violence. Compassion (Sanskrit: *karuna*) is to alleviate someone's pain, caused by their living in insecurity and fear. These are the Four Great Minds of a bodhisattva. If we practice them regularly, we will automatically be able to uproot the intention to kill. As a result, we will be determined to protect all species. We will "rid [our]selves of all weapons" and give up every form of killing. If we receive and practice this mindfulness training, energy arises in us to be of service to others. This energy arises from the intention to be humble in ourselves, to be humble before others, to love, and to have compassion.

Our own life is not isolated. It involves other people and other species. To protect nature is also to protect humanity. To protect life, we have to protect the environment and the whole of the Earth — water, air, mountains, forests, rivers, lakes, and oceans. The Buddha teaches that if we observe causes and conditions, we will be able to see that, "This is, because that is; this is not, because that is not; this is born, because that is born; this is destroyed, because that is destroyed." With this insight, we will be able to protect life in an intelligent way. The species we regard as sentient will die if we pollute the species we call insentient. The *Vajracchedika Diamond Sutra* says that the notion (notion in Sanskrit is *lakṣana*) "living being" is to be transcended. Living, or sentient, species cannot exist without non-sentient species. The boundary between sentient and non-sentient is brought about by our discriminating ideas and does not accord with things as they actually are.

If, in our life, we learn how to observe attentively and consider things deeply, we will always practice the First Mindfulness Training. It is by our practice of this mindfulness training that our planet Earth with its millions of species will have a future, and the peace and joy of all species will become a reality.

The Second Mindfulness Training —
Not To Take What Is Not Given

"Lay students of the Buddha move away from taking what has not been given, put an end to taking what has not been given. They find joy in being generous without expecting anything in return. Their minds are not obscured by greed and craving. They con-

stantly guard their own honesty and uproot from within them-
selves any intention to take what has not been given."

This mindfulness training expresses the principle of
honesty and the aspiration to bring about social justice. Like
the First Mindfulness Training, this mindfulness training
has the mind as its basis. The basis of practicing is to "uproot from within ... any intention to take what has not been
given," which means to eliminate greed by not allowing such
a state of mind to arise and obscure our understanding.
According to this mindfulness training, we practice to transform the greediness in our mind, however deep it lies in our
consciousness.

The principle and method of practicing this mindfulness
training is the principle of social justice. The Buddha teaches
his disciples to practice generosity, which is the first of the
Six Paramitas. "Paramita" means something that can take
us to the other shore — the shore of peace, joy, and liberation from suffering. "They find joy in being generous without expecting anything in return." Mahayana Buddhism lies
just under the surface of this sentence. This is the spirit of
signlessness. "Generosity" here means offering joy to someone in a way that is not characterized by the outer form. It
cannot be based on showing off, because at its source is the
heart of love and compassion. Love and compassion are
sources of energy that give us the power to practice generosity. To practice that way is to develop the ideal of a
bodhisattva that is already within us. Just as in practicing
the First Mindfulness Training we protect life, in practicing the Second Mindfulness Training we practice giving joy

motivated by generosity. Our ideal of service is a feeling of joy. That is the meaning of the sentence: "They find joy in being generous without expecting anything in return."

The objects of the practice of this mindfulness training are not only human beings, but also other living beings, including plants, trees, rocks, and the Earth. The object of our practice is not only justice in human society, but also the peace and joy of every species on Earth.

The Third Mindfulness Training —
Not To Practice Sexual Misconduct

"Lay students of the Buddha move away from sexual misconduct, put an end to sexual misconduct, and protect everyone — those under the care of their father, mother, or both father and mother; their elder sister or elder brother, their parents-in-law or other in-laws; those of the same sex; the wife, daughter, husband, or son of another; and those who have been raped, assaulted, or tortured sexually, or who are prostitutes. Lay students of the Buddha uproot from within themselves any intention to commit sexual misconduct."

This mindfulness training aims at protecting the integrity of the individual, couples, and families. Like the first two mindfulness trainings, it is first of all about the mind. If we keep this mindfulness training in our mind and our heart, we will uproot the tendency to commit sexual misconduct. If we want to protect the happiness of others, we will be able to do so effortlessly if we practice this mindfulness training in our heart. So many tragedies arise from sexual misconduct, from living in irresponsible ways. So many families have been broken by sexual misconduct; so many children have been the victims of sexual abuse. If we really consider the happiness and the future well-being of others, if we want to be able to protect them, the idea of committing sexual misconduct will not even arise in our mind.

The Fourth Mindfulness Training — Not To Lie
"Lay students of the Buddha move away from saying what is not true, put an end to saying what is not true. They say only what is true, and they find great joy in saying what is true. They always abide in truth and are completely reliable, never despising others. They have uprooted from within themselves any intention to say what is not true."

"Lay students of the Buddha put an end to saying what is not true" is explained in the words of the sutra as giving rise to a mind that "always abide[s] in truth and [is] completely reliable...." Someone who abides steadily in the truth can always be an object of the trust of others, and in that way is able to realize the work of helping others to transform very deeply. The person who observes this mindfulness training not only "move[s] away from saying what is not true, put[s] an end to saying what is not true" but also "find[s] great joy in saying what is true." The truth brings us confidence, clarity, and stability, and enlightens our path. Anyone who observes this mindfulness training not only abides in and maintains the truth, but also finds a way to make the truth more heartily accepted by others. Nevertheless the person who practices this mindfulness training is not in the least pretentious or proud. He or she does not claim to be the unique inheritor of the truth and thus can listen with great attention to what others have to say with a heart that is eager to learn. His attitude is always humble, thus the sutra says, "never despising others."

Our words can bring happiness and a feeling of confidence to others, but they can also cause suffering and damage to those around us. By practicing this mindfulness training, not only can we avoid causing suffering and damage, we give rise to feelings of confidence and offer happiness to many people at the same time. In doing this, we not only speak constructively, but we also listen attentively. Listening with great attention relieves others of their suffering. Speaking and listening are the two most important practices connected with the Fourth Mindfulness Training.

The Fifth Mindfulness Training—
Not To Use Intoxicants

"Lay students of the Buddha move away from drinking alcohol, put an end to drinking alcohol. They uproot from within themselves the habit of drinking alcohol."

Alcohol destroys our body as well as our mind. It can cause our family to break and inflict deep wounds in the hearts of young people who are born and raised in families with members who are alcoholic. In the time of the Buddha, alcohol was the common intoxicant. In our own time, there are many other intoxicants that have the capacity to cause destruction. That is why we need to aspire to uproot the habit of using intoxicants.

Alcohol and other intoxicants have broken so many families and have led to a state of chaos through many generations, bringing about much confusion in our society. To practice the Fifth Mindfulness Training is, first of all, to protect ourselves and our family. But it also gives us the opportunity of helping our society, because so many people in our society are caught in the vicious cycle of addiction. Governments are making an effort to put an end to the trafficking of drugs, but the source of addiction lies in the hearts of people. When someone feels his life has no meaning, when he feels isolated from his family and society, when there is a deep malaise within himself, he looks for a means to forget everything, and he may experiment with drugs. To stop the trafficking of drugs does not get at the heart of the problem. The lasting solution is to restore in people a feeling of confidence and faith. That is why the Buddha teaches us to practice the Four Contemplations. This practice is for us to plant faith and confidence in ourselves. It is a light that can show us the way in this life.

THE FOUR CONTEMPLATIONS

"[If] lay students of the Buddha, those who wear white robes, study and practice the Five Mindfulness Trainings and the Four Contemplations, they will realize without hardship the capacity to abide happily in the present moment. They know they will not fall into the realms of hell, hungry ghosts, animals, and other suffering paths."

The Four Contemplations are called *abhicetasika* in Pali. The Chinese understood this to mean the mind that has the capacity to develop into something beautiful. These four deep and beautiful minds are four ways to look deeply with mindfulness. In Sanskrit this kind of mindfulness practice is called anusmrti, which means mindfulness of a specific object. There is the mindfulness of the Buddha, the Dharma, the Sangha, and the Mindfulness Trainings. These mindfulness practices can ripen our faith and confidence, and bring us peace, calm, and happiness right in the present moment, giving us the energy to practice and transmit the teachings and live our ideals.

The first mindful contemplation practice is the Contemplation of the Buddha (Sanskrit: *Buddhanusmrti*):

"They practice being aware of the Buddha, meditating on the one who has come from suchness and returns to suchness; as one who is truly and fully awakened, without any attachments; as one whose understanding and practice are perfect; as the Well-Gone One; as one who knows and fully understands the world; as one who has attained the very highest; as one who has tamed what needs to be tamed; as a teacher of humans and gods; as an awakened one; and as a World-Honored One."

Tathagata is one of the titles of the Buddha. It means the one who comes from suchness and goes to suchness. Suchness (Sanskrit: *tathata*) is the wonderful nature of reality that cannot be expressed in words or ideas. The Tathagata "is truly and fully awakened, without any attachments." The Sanskrit term *"samyak sambuddha"* means "fully and perfectly awakened." A Buddha is someone who has attained the highest level of awakening and understanding and, by means of that, has arrived at the state of complete liberation. "Liberation" means to be free of the bonds of suffering which tie most living beings. Those who are liberated are free from the prisons of desire and attachment, hatred and anger, ignorance and confusion, suspicion and doubt, jealousy and pride. The Tathagata is the ideal form of a human being to which we all aspire. "One whose understanding and practice are perfect" (Sanskrit: *vidya-carana samapanna*) means that the practice and understanding of that person have reached a very deep level. The three special characteristics of perfected understanding and practice are the insight that penetrates space, the insight that penetrates time, and the insight that allows all the knots that bind us to loosen. The "Well-Gone One" (Sanskrit: *sugata*) has skillfully realized that which lies beyond birth and death and has crossed to the other shore. "One who knows and fully understands the world" (Sanskrit: *lokavid*) means someone who can penetrate the state of mind and the inner nature of all living things, sentient or insentient. Without understanding, there can be no love. It is insight that leads to love and compassion. Since a Buddha is able to penetrate the world with understanding, a Buddha is one who authentically loves the world. "One who has attained the very highest" (Sanskrit: *anuttara*) is the person who has arrived at the highest level of humanity. "One who has tamed what needs to be tamed" (Sanskrit: *purusa-damya-sarathi*) means the capacity to subdue, put in order, restrain, and train human beings, even those difficult to manage. The image here is that of a charioteer (Sanskrit: *sarathi*) who knows his horse well and is able to control him easily. "Teacher of humans and gods" (Sanskrit: *sasta-deva-manusyanam*): Gods are those whose former actions have brought them more good

practice right mindfulness is a day of increasing the light of mindfulness in ourselves. Mindfulness is a shining light, bringing joy and transforming suffering. Faith in Buddha nature is something we can touch and practice every day. This faith in our hearts is a source of great energy, called bodhicitta. It is the energy that directs our life, keeping us on the path, shining the way, and preventing us from falling into the abysses of mistakes and wrongdoing. To cultivate bodhicitta is to believe in what is most beautiful, true, and good, and most able to direct our lives. Our lives then have meaning, and we can feel this energy overflowing in us, allowing us to bring joy to others. In Mahayana Buddhism, this field of action, called "giving birth to bodhicitta," is emphasized.

"When they meditate in this way, all unwholesome desires come to an end and impure, sorrowful, and anxious elements no longer arise in their hearts. As a result of contemplating the Buddha, their thoughts are clear, they feel joy, and they arrive at the first of the Four Contemplations, abiding happily in the present moment, with ease and without any hardship."

The mindful contemplation of Buddha is a practice that can be of great benefit. It makes our faith and confidence in Buddha and in ourselves even more steady, because in ourselves there already exists the awakened nature, the capacity to wake up in understanding. When we mindfully contemplate Buddha, we have stability and feel protected, because right mindfulness is the essence of Buddha within us which has the capacity to protect us and shine light on our path. Mindfully contemplating Buddha brings joy and transforms our suffering. On his deathbed, Anathapindika felt peaceful, and the pain in his body was greatly reduced when Sariputra guided him in a meditation on the Buddha. Mindfully contemplating the Buddha is also a way of bringing out the awakened being that lies deep in us, the source of enlightened understanding that we usually call Buddhahood. Buddhists often say that Buddha is our own heart and mind.

In the Buddhist tradition there are many ways of mindfully contemplating Buddha, such as reciting the name of the Buddha or visualizing the Buddha. When we recite the name of the Buddha, we concentrate our whole mind on the name and the epithet of a Buddha, such as *Namo Sakyamunaye Buddhaya* or *Namo Amitabhaya Buddhaya*. We visualize a Buddha as one who is very serene, sitting at the foot of a tree giving teachings. At the same time, as we concentrate on the name or form of a Buddha, we also need to bear in mind that Buddha is mindfulness. The name and the form always bring to us the essence of Buddha, which is mindfulness. We should not just worship a name and a form.

To read a book on the life of the Buddha is another way of mindfully contemplating the Buddha. When we read about or listen to the life of the Buddha, we see his life, behavior, wisdom, and love clearly. As we are listening or reading in this way, the seeds of Buddhahood in our own consciousness are watered and grow. That is why we should read, listen to, and tell the story of Buddha's life many times. Everyday we can recite, "I take refuge in the Buddha, the one who shows me the way in this life," since Buddha is our refuge and protection. The practice of mindfully contemplating the Buddha gives birth to the work of realization.

The mindful contemplation of Buddha is not difficult if it is brought about by our confidence and faith. According to Buddhism, confidence is the mother who gives birth to every realization. Among the Five Powers (*pancabalani*) of the Buddhist path, the first is faith (Sanskrit: *sraddha*). After that comes the power of energy (Sanskrit: *virya*), the energy to go on. Then comes mindfulness (Sanskrit: *smrti*), right mindfulness. Fourth is the capacity to concentrate (Sanskrit: *samadhi*), meditative concentration. And fifth is insight or wisdom (Sanskrit: *prajña*). Without faith, we do not have the direction and energy to go on.

The second mindful contemplation is the Contemplation of the Dharma *(Dharmanusmrti)*:

"Lay students of the Buddha practice being aware of the Dharma, meditating as follows: the Dharma is taught by the Lord Buddha with great skill; it can lead to complete liberation; it can lead to a state of no afflictions; there is not the pain of heat in it; its value is timeless. When lay students of the Buddha meditate on and observe the Dharma in this way, all unwholesome desires come to an end, and impure, sorrowful, and anxious elements no longer arise in their hearts. As a result of contemplating the Dharma, their thoughts are clear, they feel joy, and they arrive at the second of the Four Contemplations, abiding happily in the present moment, with ease and without any hardship."

In this quote, one of the most important phrases is "abiding happily in the present moment." In Pali, it is dittha-dhamma-sukha-vihari. Practicing is not just a way of investing in the future and sacrificing the present moment. To study and practice the Dharma is to live in freedom, peace, and joy in the present moment. Then we will have freedom, peace, and joy in the future too. Someone who practices the Five Mindfulness Trainings and the Four Contemplations has happiness right in the moment. She practices without having to wait for the future. Happiness is not an empty dream on a remote horizon. It is something we can attain right away by practicing the Five Mindfulness Trainings and the Four Contemplations. That is the basic teaching of the *Sutra on the White-Clad Disciple*.

The Dharma is what a Buddha teaches—the ways of practice to arrive at awakening, peace, joy, understanding, and love. It is the path that leads to liberation. Once there is confidence in a Buddha, there is confidence in a Buddha's teachings. We contemplate mindfully the Dharma in the following way: "The Dharma is taught by the Lord Buddha with great skill." To teach skillfully is to teach beautifully. The Pali word is *svakhata*, "well-declared." Buddha is *Loka-vid*, "one who knows and understands the world." A Buddha is one who can enter the hearts of all beings with understanding and give voice to teachings that fit each being's needs. Such teachings are beautiful in the beginning, beautiful as we continue to practice them, and beautiful when we realize their fruit. "It can lead to complete liberation; it can lead to a state of no afflictions; there is not the pain of heat in it." This teaching has the capacity to relieve and transform suffering, and it also has the capacity to lead to nirvana, a state with no heat in it, when every root of affliction is transformed and we feel cool in complete liberation.

"Its value is timeless." These teachings transcend space and time, because their essential nature is the very source of life. The Dharma is not a doctrine applicable only to a certain period of history or a certain place in the world. In Sanskrit it is called *akalika,* "timeless," "not caught in time." In the Pali version we read in addition: "This Dharma can be seen right here and now. It has the capacity to lead us on the path and be directly experienced. Someone who has the insight to look into it when he hears it, can understand it of himself."

"This Dharma can be seen right here and now," *samditthika* in Pali, means that we can be directly in contact with both the content and the value of this teaching. "It has the capacity to lead us on the path," *opanayika* in Pali, means we have the capacity to return to ourselves and realize liberation. It has to be "directly experienced," *ehipassika* in Pali, means literally, "Come and see!" There is no need for an intermediary. "Someone who has the insight to look into it when he hears it, can understand it of himself," *paccatam veditabbho vinnu-hiti* in Pali, means that we can use our own cognition and insight to witness and understand the Dharma. We do not need any intermediary or authority.

Mindfully contemplating the Dharma is as important as mindfully contemplating the Buddha, because the Dharma is the way to realize the awakening that gives rise to Buddha. Dharma is the essence of Buddha. There are schools who recite the name and the epithets of the Dharma, for example the Nichiren School in Japan recites the phrase *"Namo Myo Ho Renge Kyo,"* which means "Homage to the Wonderful Mahayana *Lotus Sutra.*" Paying respect to, learning about, and observing the Dharma is no less effective than mindfully contemplating the Buddha.

Whenever we read, recite, or study the sutras, the mindfulness trainings, or the commentaries, we are mindfully contemplating the Dharma and watering Dharma seeds in our consciousness. Our life will go in a healthy direction and our wisdom will develop. As healthy seeds are watered, unwholesome seeds will gradually be transformed. That is why the sutra says: "When lay students of the Buddha meditate on and observe the Dharma in this way, all unwholesome desires come to an end, and impure, sorrowful, and anxious elements no longer arise in their hearts." Dharma is also our refuge. Every day we should recite, "I take refuge in the Dharma, the way of understanding and love." Understanding is awakened understanding, and love is compassion and loving kindness. Understanding and love are the very essence of Buddhism, the ground on which our practice resides. They are not ideas we can grasp by study alone.

The third mindful contemplation is the Contemplation of the Sangha (Sanskrit: *Sanghanusmrti*).

"Sariputra, the lay students of the Buddha practice being aware of the Sangha, meditating as follows: the noble community of the Tathagata is advancing on the right direction, it is on the path of righteousness, it is oriented towards the Dharma, and lives the teachings in the way they are meant to be lived. In that community, there are the Four Pairs and the Eight Grades — realized Arhats and those who are realizing the fruit of Arhatship, non-returners and those who are realizing the fruit of non-returning, once-returners and those who are realizing the fruit of once-returning, and stream-enterers and those who are realizing the fruit of stream-entry. The noble community of the Tathagata has successfully realized the practice of the precepts (sila), the practice

of concentration (samadhi), and the practice of insight (prajña).
It has liberation and liberated vision. It is worthy of respect, honor,
service, and offerings. It is a beautiful field of merit in our lives.
As a result of contemplating the Sangha, their thoughts are clear,
they feel joy, and they arrive at the third of the Four Contempla-
tions, abiding happily in the present moment, with ease and with-
out any hardship."

Sangha is the community of those who follow the teachings of the Buddha and know how to live in harmony and
awareness. It is sometimes translated as "noble community."
Sangha is not a community for monks and nuns alone, but
also includes the "white-clad" laypeople, who observe the
Five Mindfulness Trainings and the Four Contemplations.
A Sangha is made up of four elements: monks, nuns, laywomen, and laymen. A monk or a nun who practices with
diligence will realize the fruit of the practice, and it is exactly the same for a layperson.

"[T]he noble community of the Tathagata is advancing
on the right direction." A noble community is one committed to the practice. In the life of the community, the Buddha and the Dharma are present. This is an authentic
Sanghakaya (Sangha body) because the essence of the
Buddhakaya (Buddha body), awakening, and the essence
of the Dharmakaya (Dharma body), liberation, produce the
essence of the Sanghakaya, noble wholesomeness. To be advancing on a right direction (Pali: *supatipanna*) is to be practicing in the direction of liberation and awakening. The
noble community of the Tathagata is on the path of righteousness (Pali: *ujupatipanna*), not losing one's way in unwholesome practice, which means any practice that does not

aim at love and understanding. The noble community of the Tathagata is "oriented towards the Dharma," and practices according to the teachings (Pali: *ñayapatipanno*). It means that the practice is in accord with an ideal and does not fall behind that ideal. The noble community of the Tathagata "lives the teachings in the way they are meant to be lived" (Pali: *ɗamicipatipanna*) means that the teachings are not only expressed in words but more so in the way the practitioners live them. "In that community, there are the Four Pairs and the Eight Grades—realized Arhats and those who are realizing the fruit of Arhatship, non-returners and those who are realizing the fruit of non-returning, once-returners and those who are realizing the fruit of once-returning, and stream-enterers and those who are realizing the fruit of stream-entry." Arhat is the level of realizing there is no birth and death. It is also the level of having transformed all the roots of affliction. One who realizes the fruit of non-returning (Pali: *anagamin*) realizes there is no need to return to be caught in the suffering and bondage of the desire realm, but only needs to return one more time to the form or the formless realm in order to realize the fruit of Arhatship. Once-returner (Pali: *ɗakrɗagamin*) only needs to return once more to the desire realm before realizing the fruit of Arhatship. A stream-enterer (Pali: *ɗrotapanna*) is one who has entered the noble stream and needs to return only seven times to the desire realm before becoming an Arhat. These are the people who steadily practice the Five Mindfulness Trainings and the Four Contemplations. Once the state of Arhatship is reached, it is called the fruit of Arhatship. Someone who is on the way to Arhatship is said to be moving in the direction of becoming an Arhat. Thus there is the fruit of non-returning and the direction of non-returning, the fruit of once-returning and the direction of once-returning, the fruit of stream-entry and the direction of stream-entry. The different levels of fruit and direction are called the Four Pairs and the Eight Grades (Pali: *cattari purisa-sayugani, attha purisa-puggala*). Anyone who participates in the life of the community will belong to one of the eight grades.

"The noble community of the Tathagata has successfully realized... the practice of the precepts *(sila)*." These trainings are simply a manifestation of a life lived mindfully. Mindfulness Trainings protect us by preventing us from getting lost on the path. They nourish the power of concentration. That is why the sutra says, "The noble community of the Tathagata has successfully realized the practice of concentration *(samadhi)*." Samadhi is meditative concentration. "The noble community of the Tathagata has successfully realized... the practice of insight. It has liberation and liberated vision." Insight (Sanskrit: *prajña*) is the understanding that is able to lead to liberation (Sanskrit: *vimukti*), or freeing ourselves from that which binds us. "Liberated vision" means there are certain things that we can only see and hear once we are free—the nature of no birth and no death, no coming and no going, no one and no many, no permanence and no annihilation, namely, the experience of nirvana itself.

The noble community of the Tathagata is "worthy of respect, honor, service, and offerings. It is a beautiful field of merit in our lives." To respect, honor, serve, and support

communities that study and practice is an intelligent investment that can be of great benefit to the world. The Sangha
body is a fertile field in which we can sow our most precious
seeds. There is no field more beautiful for sowing the seeds
of happiness than the practice community. It is called the
highest field of merit (Pali: *anuttara punna-khetta*).

If we practice without a Sangha body, it is very difficult
for us to succeed. The Sangha body is our source of inspi-
ration and comfort, and our refuge. When we feel discour-
aged and fatigued, our Sangha body will give us renewed
strength, because there is always someone there who practices diligently, with insight, compassion, and freshness. In
Vietnam, we say that a monk who leaves his practice community is like a tiger who leaves his mountain. If the tiger
leaves his mountain to come down to the plains, it will be
caught and killed by men. The practitioner will give up the
practice too easily if he or she is without a Sangha. That is
why we take refuge in the Sangha: "I take refuge in the
Sangha, the community that lives in harmony and awareness." The special qualities of the Sangha are its harmony
and its mindfulness. It is our job to keep this special quality at a high level. We should not say that this quality is not
high enough as an excuse for leaving the Sangha. We should
practice to bring this special quality to its highest level.

Good practitioners always keep Sangha-building in mind.
Sangha-building is the work of months and years. If the
Sangha body is in good health then the practice and the
transformation of everyone who comes into that community
will come easily and quickly. Let us not be taken in by the
saying, "When he practices, he attains realization, and when

she practices she attains realization." We have to pool our strength in order to build a Sangha.

By mindful contemplation of Buddha, Dharma, and Sangha, we can give rise to the true roots of the Three Jewels in ourselves. The real Buddha is made of awakened understanding, love, and compassion. The true Buddha is not a deity who hands out merits and demerits. The true teachings can be studied and practiced, always taking into account impermanence, selflessness, and nirvana. The true teachings are not the way of superstition. The true community is built on the foundations of mindfulness trainings, concentration, and insight as well as openness, freshness, and happiness. A true Sangha is not one that struggles for fame and profit. In a true Sangha, there are always the marks of the true Buddha and the true Dharma.

The fourth mindful contemplation is the Contemplation of the Mindfulness Trainings (Sanskrit: *Silanusmrti*).

"[T]he lay students of the Buddha practice being mindful of the Mindfulness Trainings, meditating as follows: the Mindfulness Trainings have no drawbacks, no flaws, no impurities, and no unsound points; and they help us abide in the land of the Tathagata. The Mindfulness Trainings are not of the nature to deceive. They are always praised, accepted, practiced, and guarded by the holy ones. As a result of contemplating the Mindfulness Trainings, the students' thoughts are clear, they feel joy, and they arrive at the fourth of the Four Contemplations, abiding happily in the present moment, with ease and without any hardship."

The mindfulness trainings, as we have already seen, are the manifestation of a mindful life. Mindfulness trainings are not laws that others force us to keep. It is we ourselves who have the deep aspiration to live in accord with them. Because we are living in mindfulness, we decide to receive and observe the mindfulness trainings as the most skillful way to protect ourselves and help us succeed in the practice. For example, when we see the suffering and all the fear brought about by killing, we are determined to receive the mindfulness training not to kill. By practicing this mindfulness training, we protect ourselves and we also protect all living beings. At the same time, we give our love and our compassion a chance to grow. This mindfulness training was proposed by the Buddha and since then has been practiced and clarified by many generations of Buddhists. Mindfulness trainings are not superstitious abstinence with some mystical effect that is impossible for us to understand. Mindfulness trainings are based on mindfulness, awakened insight, love, and compassion. That is why "the Mindfulness Trainings have no drawbacks, no flaws, no impurities, and no unsound points." Mindfulness trainings must be practiced intelligently; we can see in the mindfulness trainings the Buddha, the Dharma, and the Sangha. The mindfulness trainings are also as deep, lovely, and holy as the Buddha, the Dharma, and the Sangha. To have confidence and faith in the mindfulness trainings is also to have confidence and faith in the Buddha, the Dharma, and the Sangha, because the mindfulness trainings are the essence of the Three Jewels.

Mindfulness Trainings "help us abide in the land of the Tathagata." This must be one of the most beautiful sentences in the sutra. The domain of the Tathagata is a place of security, peace, and joy, illuminated by love and understanding. By practicing the mindfulness trainings, we enter the domain of the Tathagata, which is the abode of love, compassion, joy, and impartiality (the Four Unlimited Minds). To observe the mindfulness trainings is also to contemplate mindfully the Buddha, the Dharma, and the Sangha. In each of the mindfulness trainings is contained the Buddha, the Dharma, and the Sangha.

"The Mindfulness Trainings are not of the nature to deceive," because they are founded on the basis of mindfulness, awakened understanding, love, and compassion. Anyone can understand them and directly experience the fruit of practicing them. No one can succeed in meditative concentration and insight without the practice of the mindfulness trainings. That is why "they are always praised, accepted, practiced, and guarded by the holy ones." Guarding the mindfulness trainings means that we ourselves practice them and thus become an example for others in their practice. As a result, the practice of the mindfulness trainings has been adopted widely in many different parts of the world. Just as when we drive a car and follow the rules of the highway to avoid causing an accident and to allow others to arrive at their destination safely, in our everyday lives we practice the mindfulness trainings to protect ourselves and others and to arrive at our destination of realizing our ideal of liberation and awakening. Practicing the Five Mindfulness Trainings and the Four Contemplations, we are able to live happily right away. We know that we will not fall into unwholesome and unhappy paths in the future. The phrase, "abiding happily in the present moment," is repeated six times in the sutra. Many people think that the practice must be difficult if they are to succeed in the future, even though the Buddha taught very clearly in many discourses that the practice of his teachings brings peace and joy in the present and peace and joy in the future. According to the Buddha, when we have real peace and joy in the present (which does not mean a life of mindless indulgence in sensual pleasures), it will always lead to peace and joy in the future. If we want to see the future, we need only look at the present. Knowing that she is steadily practicing the Five Mindfulness Trainings and the Four Contemplations, the practitioner dressed in the white robe is aware that she has already entered the noble stream and holds the fruit of stream-entry, which means she will not fall again into hell, hungry-ghost, and animal realms.

In many sutras, the Buddha teaches us to live in the present moment and mindfully observe everything that arises in the present moment. If we abandon the present, if we distance ourselves from the present in order to daydream confusedly about the past or future, we are doing the opposite of what the Awakened Ones taught. To practice the Five Mindfulness Trainings and the Four Contemplations is to practice taking hold of our fate in the present moment, protecting the present, building the present, and guaranteeing the future. The way to bring about the best future is to live deeply, responsibly, in an awakened way, with love and understanding, in the present moment. The Buddha also taught that liberation, peace, joy, awakening, and the Pure Land are to be found within our own mind, and that only when we return to ourselves can we discover and illuminate those precious gems and be truly in touch with them. We can only throw light on something in the present moment. To live peacefully and happily in the present moment is an important message from the Buddha, but it seems that this message has been forgotten to a great extent in the circles of Buddhist practice.

To live happily in the present moment according to the teachings of the Awakened One is not something so very difficult to do. The Buddha teaches that if we practice the Five Mindfulness Trainings and the Four Contemplations, that is already enough. By practicing these things, we have peace and joy in the present moment, "with ease and without any hardship."

In the verse portion of the sutra, the Buddha teaches:

> *But the truly virtuous men and women*
> *are those who practice the*
> *Wonderful Mindfulness Trainings*
> *and are able to realize liberation.*
> *Like the Well-Gone One, they live in true freedom.*

This verse touches on the subject of Sangha-building. Since the Sangha body is a field of merit, we have to look at its qualities to determine whether it is one we should invest in and practice with. The criteria are liberation and awakening. Any Sangha body that has members who seriously and joyfully practice the mindfulness trainings and realize liberation is a Sangha body of high quality that should be supported and can be a refuge. The value of these members lies in their pure practice of the mindfulness trainings and their liberation, and not in their family backgrounds or their castes or social status. Even if they come from a noble background, if they do not practice the mindfulness trainings and do not have liberation, they are not of great value to the Sangha jewel:

> *In our human world,*
> *there are Brahmans, warriors,*
> *scholars, tradesmen,*
> *and artisans.*

> *There is no need to discriminate*
> *according to family or caste.*
> *To realize the greatest happiness*
> *is to make offerings to those who are truly virtuous.*

> *A person who lacks in virtue*
> *or is poor in insight*
> *cannot light the way for others.*
> *To make offerings to such a one*
> *bears little fruit.*

> *Sons and daughters of Buddha*
> *who practice the way of insight*
> *and have their minds directed to Buddha*
> *have strong, stable roots*
> *and are reborn only to be happy.*

Brahman means one who comes from the priestly caste. *Kṣatriya* denotes the warrior class (generals and politicians). Buddha gives the example of a herd of oxen to explain the value of the Sangha body. The value of an ox did not lie in its color or place of origin. Its value resided in its ability to pull loads. Any ox that was strong and healthy and able to pull a cart strongly and quickly, and could do so for many loads, had value.

> *Look carefully at the herd*
> *of oxen over there.*
>
> *Some oxen are white and yellow.*
> *Some are black or red.*
> *Some are brown with yellow spots,*
> *while others are grey like pigeons.*
>
> *Whatever their color*
> *or place of origin,*
> *their value to us lies*
> *in their ability to transport.*
>
> *Healthy and strong ones*
> *who pull carts vigorously,*
> *can make many journeys*
> *and are the most useful.*

CONCLUSION

The *Sutra on the White-Clad Disciple* is basic for our practice, not just for the practice of laypersons but also for the practice of monks and nuns. When we put the teachings of this sutra into practice, we see the interconnectedness of the Five Mindfulness Trainings and the Four Contemplations. When we practice one mindfulness training very deeply, we are also practicing all the other mindfulness trainings. When we observe the First Mindfulness Training—not to kill—we see that if we do not practice the other four mindfulness trainings, there is no way we can truly and deeply practice the First Mindfulness Training. The acts of stealing, sexual misconduct, irresponsible speech, and using of alcohol and drugs lead also to the killing of living beings. If we practice one of the Four Contemplations very deeply, we see that we are able to practice the other three. When we practice mindful contemplation of the Buddha, we see that we are also practicing mindful contemplation of the Dharma, the Sangha, and the Mindfulness Trainings. Each contemplation contains within itself the other three. What is more, each of the Five Mindfulness Trainings contains the essence of Buddha, Dharma, and Sangha, and each of the Four Contemplations contains all Five Mindfulness Trainings. The essence of the Five Mindfulness Trainings and the Four Contemplations is right mindfulness, awakened understanding, love, and compassion. Each of these practices interpenetrates the others. The *Avatamsaka Sutra* talks about this truth as "interbeing" and "interpenetration."

At the moment Shakyamuni Buddha realized awakening at the foot of the *bodhi* tree, he said, "How strange! All living beings have the awakened quality and loving compassion in their hearts, but they cannot see it and they continue to go on the round of birth and death. This gives rise to great compassion." Faith in Buddhism is faith in the nature of awakening, the capacity to wake up that which is available within us. Awakening is the most beautiful, wholesome, and real thing to do. The Buddha invites us to be in contact with that nature of awakening. When we begin the practice of conscious breathing, we are already in contact with mindfulness. When we mindfully contemplate Buddha, Dharma, Sangha, and the Mindfulness Trainings, we are already in contact with mindfulness, and our own nature of awakening becomes the basis of our life. Mindfulness leads to clear vision. Clear vision is awakening itself. The source of awakening is the awakening nature in us. Buddha is a person who has the awakening nature in herself perfectly developed. Someone who practices according to the Buddha's teachings is in the process of developing the awakening nature in himself. The Buddha does not ask us to believe in a creator god or a metaphysical first principle. The object of our faith and confidence must be something real, something we can touch. Mindfulness and awakened understanding are real. The Five Mindfulness Trainings and the Four Contemplations are the way mindfulness expresses itself. The Five Mindfulness Trainings and the Four Contemplations are ways of practice that give rise to mindfulness and awakened understanding. This is the object of faith in Buddhism.

Faith (Sanskrit: *sraddha*) is the source of the energy necessary for practicing the teachings and imparting them to others. Faith leads to eager perseverance and, as a result, we have mindfulness that takes us on to concentration and the arising of the insight called awakened understanding. The insight of awakened understanding in turn allows our faith to be even greater. Faith, energy, mindfulness, concentration, and insight are the five sources of energy we need to succeed on the path of learning the practice. The *Sutra on the White-Clad Disciple* expounds the method of practicing the Five Mindfulness Trainings and the Four Contemplations as the objects of our faith.

Human beings cannot live happily and meaningfully without something true, wholesome, and beautiful to believe in. Without faith, we live with no sense of responsibility, and we destroy our own bodies, our souls, our families, and our society. Our own time is an era of lost faith. People have lost faith in God, science, ideals, and ideologies. The older generation wants their children to accept their own faith, but that faith is often vague, and many of them themselves have no steady grasp of it. That is why they are unable to expound the essence of faith so that the younger generation can understand, see, and accept it. In the Pali version of the *Sutra on the White-Clad Disciple,* the Buddha says quite clearly, "The teachings can be seen here right now, their function is to direct in the best direction. They can be approached in order to be directly experienced and someone who has the wisdom to examine them can, by listening to them, understand them." The *Sutra on the White-Clad Disciple* does not have any secret or ambiguous hidden meaning in it. Everything the sutra teaches is tangible; it can be touched and experienced. To learn, study, practice, and expound this sutra can help young people see their own awakened nature, and they can take this as the object of their faith. The teachings of the Buddha are only to help us give birth to this faith. Once faith has arisen, we have a new source of energy within us, and with this energy we can live with joy, freshness, and happiness in each moment, knowing how to protect body, mind, and soul, and build a new family and a new society. Our life will begin to have meaning.

All spiritual and religious traditions have the responsibility of initiating and helping develop faith. If we are stuck in old ways of seeing things, we are not able to carry out this responsibility. The people who represent and take responsibility for religious traditions should look at this very carefully. They should not, in the name of tradition, force the younger generation to accept things they cannot experience for themselves, because this will make them turn away from those things altogether. Ours is a scientific age. We cannot force young people to believe in vague, abstract ideas that they cannot experience directly. We need to go back to something deep in our traditions and rediscover the best values that have been buried under countless layers of rigid forms. Only then will we have the insight and the language to express the true objects of our faith and confidence.

The Dharma is a living reality. Like a great tree that is always growing, Buddhism continues to develop. The Five Mindfulness Trainings are sources of faith and confidence that are still alive and that we can practice wholeheartedly in our own times, in our daily lives.

PART FIVE

Ceremonies

Tranmission of the Three Jewels and the Five Mindfulness Trainings

INCENSE OFFERING

In gratitude, we offer this incense to all Buddhas and bodhisattvas throughout space and time. May it be fragrant as Earth herself, reflecting our careful efforts, our whole-hearted awareness, and the fruit of understanding, slowly ripening in us. May we and all beings be companions of Buddhas and bodhisattvas. May we awaken from forgetfulness and realize our true home.

(bell)

TOUCHING THE EARTH

Bringing light in to the Ten Directions, the Buddha, the Dharma, and the Sangha, to whom we bow in gratitude.

(bell)

Teaching and living the way of awareness in the very midst of suffering and confusion, Shakyamuni Buddha, the Enlightened One, to whom we bow in gratitude.

(bell)

Cutting through ignorance, awakening our hearts and minds, Manjushri, the Bodhisattva of Great Understanding, to whom we bow in gratitude.

(bell)

Working mindfully and joyfully for the sake of all beings, Samantabhadra, the Bodhisattva of Great Action, to whom we bow in gratitude.

(bell)

Responding to suffering, serving beings in countless ways, Avalokitesvara, the Bodhisattva of Great Compassion, to whom we bow in gratitude.

(bell)

Seed of awakening and loving kindness in children and all beings, Maitreya, the Buddha To Be Born, to whom we bow in gratitude.

(bell)

Showing the way fearlessly and compassionately, the stream of ancestral teachers, to whom we bow in gratitude.

(two sounds of the bell)

OPENING CHANT

(Head of Ceremony chants each line, echoed by whole assembly):

The Dharma is deep and lovely.
We now have a chance to see it,
study it, and practice it.
We vow to realize its true meaning.

THE HEART OF THE PRAJÑAPARAMITA

The Bodhisattva Avalokita,
While moving in the deep course of perfect understanding,
Shed light on the five skandhas
And found them equally empty.
After this penetration, he overcame ill-being.

(bell)

Listen, Sariputra,
Form is emptiness, emptiness is form.
Form is not other than emptiness.
Emptiness is not other than form.
The same is true with feelings,
Perceptions, mental formations, and consciousness.

(bell)

Hear, Sariputra,
All dharmas are marked with emptiness.
They are neither produced nor destroyed,
Neither defiled nor immaculate,
Neither increasing nor decreasing.
Therefore in emptiness there is neither form,
Nor feelings, nor perceptions,
Nor mental formations, nor consciousness;
No eye, or ear, or nose, or tongue, or body, or mind;
No form, no sound, no smell, no taste, no touch, no object
of mind;
No realms of elements (from eyes to mind consciousness);
No interdependent origins and no extinction of them
(From ignorance to death and decay);

No ill-being, no cause of ill-being,
No end of ill-being, and no path;
No understanding, no attainment.

(bell)

Because there is no attainment,
The bodhisattvas, grounded in perfect understanding,
Find no obstacles for their minds.
Having no obstacles, they overcome fear,
Liberating themselves forever from illusion
And realizing perfect nirvana.
All Buddhas in the past, present, and future,
Thanks to this perfect understanding,
Arrive at full, right, and universal enlightenment.

(bell)

Therefore one should know that perfect understanding
Is the highest mantra, the unequaled mantra,
The destroyer of ill-being, the incorruptible truth.
A mantra of prajñaparamita should therefore be pro-
claimed.

This is the mantra:

> *Gate gate paragate*
> *Paraѕamgate*
> *Boдhi Svaha.*

(three sounds of the bell)

SANGHAKARMAN PROCEDURE

Sanghakarman Master: Has the whole community assembled?

Sanghakarman Convener: The whole community has assembled.

Sanghakarman Master: Is there harmony in the community?

Sanghakarman Convener: Yes, there is harmony.

Sanghakarman Master: Why has the community assembled?

Sanghakarman Convener: The community has assembled to perform the sanghakarman of transmitting the Three Jewels and the Five Mindfulness Trainings.

Sanghakarman Master: Noble community, today, (date), has been chosen as the day to transmit the Three Jewels and the Five Mindfulness Trainings. The Community has assembled at the appointed time and is ready to transmit and receive the Three Jewels and Five Mindfulness Trainings in an atmosphere of harmony. Thus, the tranmission can proceed. Is that correct?

Everyone: That is correct.

(repeat question and answer three times)

BOWING IN GRATITUDE

In gratitude to their fathers and mothers who gave them birth, the ordinees bow deeply before the Three Jewels in the Ten Directions.

(bell)

In gratitude to their teachers who have shown them how to love, understand, and abide happily in the present moment, the ordinees bow deeply before the Three Jewels in the Ten Directions.

(bell)

In gratitude to friends who guide them on the path and offer support in difficult moments, the ordinees bow deeply before the Three Jewels in the Ten Directions.

(two sounds of the bell)

INTRODUCTORY WORDS

Today the community has gathered to give spiritual support to our brothers and sisters ___(names)___ who will go for refuge to the Three Jewels and take the vow to practice the Five Mindfulness Trainings. Will the entire community please enjoy your breathing and remain mindful when you hear the three sounds of the bell. The sound of the bell is the voice of the Buddha, bringing us back to our true selves.

(three sounds of the bell)

TRANSMISSION OF THE THE THREE JEWELS

Today the community has gathered to give support to those who will vow to go for refuge to the Three Jewels and receive and practice the Five Mindfulness Trainings. You have had the chance to learn about and observe the way of understanding and love that has been handed down to us by teachers over many centuries, and today you have made the decision to go for refuge to the Three Jewels and receive the Five Mindfulness Trainings.

To take refuge in the Three Jewels is to turn to the Buddha, the Dharma, and the Sangha for protection. The Buddha, the Dharma, and the Sangha are three precious gems. To take refuge in the Buddha is to take refuge in an awakened person who has the ability to show us the way in this life. To take refuge in the Dharma is to take refuge in the way of understanding, love, and compassion. To take refuge in the Sangha is to take refuge in a community that practices according to the path of understanding, love, and compassion and lives in an awakened way.

The Buddha, the Dharma, and the Sangha are present in every quarter of the universe as well as in every person and all other species. To go for refuge to the Buddha, the Dharma, and the Sangha also means to have confidence in our own ability to be awakened, to develop and manifest understanding and love in ourselves, and to practice the way for ourselves and for the community. Will the ordinees please repeat after me the Three Great Refuge Vows:

> *I take refuge in the Buddha,*
> *the one who shows me the way in this life.*

> (bell)

> *I take refuge in the Dharma,*
> *the way of understanding and love.*

> (bell)

> *I take refuge in the Sangha,*
> *the community that lives in harmony and awareness.*

Thich Nhat Hanh

(bell)

CONCLUDING WORDS

Brothers and Sisters, you have formally received the Three Refuges in order to see the Three Jewels in your own heart and bring them into your daily life. Today you have become students of the Awakened One and have made the vow to live an awakened life. Beginning from today you will apply your mind to learning about and practicing the way of understanding, love, and compassion, which means to nourish the ability to love and understand within ourselves. You will also go for refuge to your Sangha in order to learn and practice, and you will attend days and retreats of mindfulness and recitations of the trainings and other activities of your Sangha. The transmitter of the Refuges to you is   (name of transmitter)   , and your Dharma name will be chosen by him or her. You should take refuge in your teacher and your Sangha to learn and practice the path.

TRANSMISSION OF THE FIVE MINDFULNESS TRAININGS

Ordinees, now is the time to transmit the Five Mindfulness Trainings. The Five Mindfulness Trainings have the capacity to protect life and make it beautiful. The Five Mindfulness Trainings encourage us in the direction of peace, joy, liberation, and awakening. They are the foundation for individual happiness and the happiness of the family and society. If we practice according to the Five Mindfulness Trainings, we are already on the path of right practice. The Five Mindfulness Trainings protect us and help us avoid making mistakes and creating suffering, fear, and despair. Practicing the Five Trainings, we are able to build peace and happiness in ourselves and our family, and joy and peace in our society.

I will now recite the Five Mindfulness Trainings. Listen carefully with a calm and clear mind. Say, "Yes, I do" every time you see you have the capacity to receive, learn, and practice the training read.

Brothers and Sisters, are you ready?

Ordinees: Yes, we are ready.

This is the First Mindfulness Training:
Aware of the suffering caused by the destruction of life, I am committed to cultivating compassion and learning ways to protect the lives of people, animals, plants, and minerals. I am determined not to kill, not to let others kill, and not to condone any act of killing in the world, in my thinking, and in my way of life.

This is the first of the Five Mindfulness Trainings. Do you vow to receive, study, and practice it?

Ordinees: Yes, I do.

(bell)

This is the Second Mindfulness Training:
Aware of the suffering caused by exploitation, social injustice, stealing, and oppression, I am committed to cultivating loving kindness and learning ways to work for the well-being of people, animals, plants, and minerals. I will practice generosity by sharing my time, energy, and material resources with those who are in real need. I am determined not to steal and not to possess anything that should belong to others. I will respect the property of others, but I will prevent others from profiting from human suffering or the suffering of other species on Earth.

This is the second of the Five Mindfulness Trainings. Do you vow to receive, study, and practice it?

Ordinees: Yes, I do.

(bell)

This is the Third Mindfulness Training:
Aware of the suffering caused by sexual misconduct, I am committed to cultivating responsibility and learning ways to protect the safety and integrity of individuals, couples, families, and society. I am determined not to engage in sexual relations without love and a long-term commitment. To preserve the happiness of myself and others, I am determined to respect my commitments and the commitments of others. I will do everything in my power to protect children from sexual abuse and to prevent couples and families from being broken by sexual misconduct.

This is the third of the Five Mindfulness Trainings. Do you vow to receive, study, and practice it?

Ordinees: Yes, I do.

(bell)

This is the Fourth Mindfulness Training:
Aware of the suffering caused by unmindful speech and the inability to listen to others, I am committed to cultivating loving speech and deep listening in order to bring joy and happiness to others and relieve others of their suffering. Knowing that words can create happiness or suffering, I am determined to speak truthfully, with words that inspire self-confidence, joy, and hope. I will not spread news that I do not know to be certain and will not criticize or condemn things of which I am not sure. I will refrain from uttering words that can cause division or discord, or that can cause the family or the community to break. I am determined to make all efforts to reconcile and resolve all conflicts, however small.

This is the fourth of the Five Mindfulness Trainings. Do you vow to receive, study, and practice it?

Ordinees: Yes, I do.

(bell)

This is the Fifth Mindfulness Training:

Aware of the suffering caused by unmindful consumption, I am committed to cultivating good health, both physical and mental, for myself, my family, and my society by practicing mindful eating, drinking, and consuming. I will ingest only items that preserve peace, well-being, and joy in my body, in my consciousness, and in the collective body and consciousness of my family and society. I am determined not to use alcohol or any other intoxicant or to ingest foods or other items that contain toxins, such as certain TV programs, magazines, books, films, and conversations. I am aware that to damage my body or my consciousness with these poisons is to betray my ancestors, my parents, my society, and future generations. I will work to transform violence, fear, anger, and confusion in myself and in society by practicing a diet for myself and for society. I understand that a proper diet is crucial for self-transformation and for the transformation of society.

This is the fifth of the Five Mindfulness Trainings. Do you vow to receive, study, and practice it?

Ordinees: Yes, I do.

(bell)

Brothers and Sisters, you have received the Five Mindfulness Trainings which are the foundation of happiness in the family and in society. They are the basis for the aspiration to help others. You should recite the trainings often, at least once a month, so that your understanding and practice of the Five Mindfulness Trainings can grow deeper every day.

A trainings recitation ceremony can be organized in the practice center or at home with friends. If you do not recite the trainings at least once in three months, you lose the transmission and today's ceremony will be nullified. Brothers and Sisters, as students of the Buddha you should be energetic in practicing the way the Buddha has taught to create peace and happiness for yourselves and all species. Upon hearing the sound of the bell, please stand up and bow deeply three times to show your gratitude to the Three Jewels.

(three sounds of the bell)

READING THE TRAININGS CERTIFICATE

Brothers and Sisters, I will now read the trainings certificate.

(The transmitter of the trainings reads the certificate on which is written the Dharma name of the ordinee and the name of his or her teacher. Each ordinee kneels in order while listening to the reading of his or her certificate, after which the certificate is given to him or her.)

RECITATION IN SUPPORT OF THE ORDINEES

Noble community, to lend spiritual support to our brothers and sisters who have been ordained, please recite the Three Refuges in mindfulness:

Buddham saranam gacchami.
Dharmam saranam gacchami.
Sangham saranam gacchami.

CLOSING CHANT

Please join your palms and recite each line of the closing chant after me:

Transmitting the trainings, practicing the way of awareness
gives rise to benefits without limit.
I vow to share the fruits with all beings.
I vow to offer tribute to parents, teachers,
friends, and numerous beings
who give guidance and support along the path.

Recitation Ceremony
of the Three Jewels, the Two Promises, and the Five Mindfulness Trainings

THREE JEWELS AND TWO PROMISES: RECITATION FOR CHILDREN

INCENSE OFFERING

Head of Ceremony: In gratitude, we offer this incense to all Buddhas and bodhisattvas throughout space and time. May it be fragrant as Earth herself, reflecting our careful efforts, our wholehearted awareness, and the fruit of understanding, slowly ripening in us. May we and all beings be companions of Buddhas and bodhisattvas. May we awaken from forgetfulness and realize our true home.

(bell)

TOUCHING THE EARTH

Teaching and living the way of awareness in the very midst of suffering and confusion, Shakyamuni Buddha, the Enlightened One, to whom we bow in gratitude.

(bell)

Cutting through ignorance, awakening our hearts and minds, Manjushri, the Bodhisattva of Great Understanding, to whom we bow in gratitude.

(bell)

Working mindfully and joyfully for the sake of all beings, Samantabhadra, the Bodhisattva of Great Action, to whom we bow in gratitude.

(bell)

Responding to suffering, serving beings in countless ways, Avalokitesvara, the Bodhisattva of Great Compassion, to whom we bow in gratitude.

(bell)

Seed of awakening and loving kindness in children and all beings, Maitreya, the Buddha To Be Born, to whom we bow in gratitude.

(bell)

Showing the way fearlessly and compassionately, the stream of ancestral teachers, to whom we bow in gratitude.

(two sounds of the bell)

OPENING CHANT

(Head of Ceremony chants each line, echoed by whole assembly):

The Dharma is deep and lovely.
We now have a chance to see it,
study it, and practice it.
We vow to realize its true meaning.

Today the community has gathered to recite the Three Jewels, the Two Promises, the Five Mindfulness Trainings, and the Fourteen Mindfulness Trainings of the Order of Interbeing. First we will recite the Three Jewels and the Two Promises. Will the younger members of the community please come forward.

Young people, upon hearing the sound of the bell, please bow three times to show your gratitude to the Buddha, the Dharma, and the Sangha.

(bell)

THE THREE JEWELS

Young students of the Buddha, you have taken refuge in the Buddha, the one who shows you the way in this life; in the Dharma, the way of understanding and love; and in the Sangha, the community that lives in harmony and awareness. It is beneficial to recite the Three Jewels regularly. Will the entire community please join with the young people in repeating after me:

> *I take refuge in the Buddha,*
> *the one who shows me the way in this life.*
> *I take refuge in the Dharma,*
> *the way of understanding and love.*
> *I take refuge in the Sangha,*
> *the community that lives in harmony and awareness.*

THE TWO PROMISES

Young students of the Buddha, we have completed the recitation of the Three Jewels. Now we will recite the Two Promises that you have made with the Buddha, the Dharma, and the Sangha. Will the entire community please join the young people in repeating after me:

I vow to develop understanding,
in order to live peaceably
with people, animals, plants, and minerals.

This is the first promise you have made with the Buddha, our teacher. Have you tried to learn more about it and to keep your promise during the past two weeks?

(bell)

I vow to develop my compassion,
in order to protect the lives
of people, animals, plants, and minerals.

This is the second promise you have made with the Buddha, our teacher. Have you tried to learn more about it and to keep your promise during the past two weeks?

(bell)

Young students of the Enlightened One, understanding and love are the two most important teachings of the Buddha. If we do not make the effort to be open, to understand the suffering of other people, we will not be able to love them and to live in harmony with them. We should also try to understand and protect the lives of animals, plants, and minerals and live in harmony with them. If we cannot understand, we cannot love. The Buddha teaches us to look at living beings with the eyes of love and understanding. Please learn to practice this teaching.

Young people, upon hearing the sound of the bell, please bow three times to the Three Jewels, and then you can leave the Meditation Hall.

(three sounds of the bell)

RECITING THE FIVE MINDFULNESS TRAININGS

(This ceremony should begin with Incense Offering, Touching the Earth, and Opening Chant from pages 251-252.)

SANGHAKARMAN PROCEDURE

Sanghakarman Master: Has the entire community assembled?

Sanghakarman Convener: The entire community has assembled.

Sanghakarman Master: Is there harmony in the community?

Sanghakarman Convener: Yes, there is harmony.

Sanghakarman Master: Is there anyone not able to be present who has asked to be represented, and have they declared themselves to have done their best to study and practice the Five Mindfulness Trainings?

Sanghakarman Convener: No, there is not.

or

Sanghakarman Convener: Yes, ____(name)____, for health reasons, cannot be at the recitation today. She has asked ____(name)____ to represent her and she declares that she has done her best to study and practice the mindfulness trainings.

Sanghakarman Master: What is the reason for the community gathering today?

Sanghakarman Convener: The community has gathered to practice the recitation of the Five Mindfulness Trainings. Noble community, please listen. Today, _____(date)_____, has been declared to be the Mindfulness Trainings Recitation Day. We have gathered at the appointed time. The noble community is ready to hear and recite the mindfulness trainings in an atmosphere of harmony, and the recitation can proceed.

Is that correct?

Everyone: That is correct.

(repeat question and answer three times)

INTRODUCTORY WORDS

Brothers and Sisters, it is now time to recite the Five Mindfulness Trainings. Please, those who have been ordained as Upasaka and Upasika, kneel with joined palms in the direction of the Buddha, our teacher.

Brothers and Sisters, please listen. The Five Mindfulness Trainings are the basis for a happy life. They have the capacity to protect life and to make it beautiful and worth living. They are also the door that opens to enlightenment and liberation. Please listen to each mindfulness training, and answer yes, silently every time you see that you have made the effort to study, practice, and observe it.

THE FIVE MINDFULNESS TRAININGS

THE FIRST OF THE FIVE MINDFULNESS TRAININGS

Aware of the suffering caused by the destruction of life, I am committed to cultivating compassion and learning ways to protect the lives of people, animals, plants, and minerals. I am determined not to kill, not to let others kill, and not to condone any act of killing in the world, in my thinking, and in my way of life.

(silence)

This is the first of the Five Mindfulness Trainings. Have you made an effort to study and practice it during the past two weeks?

(bell)

THE SECOND OF THE FIVE MINDFULNESS TRAININGS

Aware of the suffering caused by exploitation, social injustice, stealing, and oppression, I am committed to cultivating loving kindness and learning ways to work for the well-being of people, animals, plants, and minerals. I will practice generosity by sharing my time, energy, and material resources with those who are in real need. I am determined not to steal and not to possess anything that should belong to others. I will respect the property of others, but I will prevent others from profiting from human suffering or the suffering of other species on Earth.

(silence)

This is the second of the Five Mindfulness Trainings. Have you made an effort to study and practice it during the past two weeks?

(bell)

THE THIRD OF THE FIVE MINDFULNESS TRAININGS

Aware of the suffering caused by sexual misconduct, I am committed to cultivating responsibility and learning ways to protect the safety and integrity of individuals, couples, families, and society. I am determined not to engage in sexual relations without love and a long-term commitment. To preserve the happiness of myself and others, I am determined to respect my commitments and the commitments of others. I will do everything in my power to protect children from sexual abuse and to prevent couples and families from being broken by sexual misconduct.

(silence)

This is the third of the Five Mindfulness Trainings. Have you made an effort to study and practice it during the past two weeks?

(bell)

THE FOURTH OF THE FIVE MINDFULNESS TRAININGS

Aware of the suffering caused by unmindful speech and the inability to listen to others, I am committed to cultivating loving speech and deep listening in order to bring joy and happiness to others and relieve others of their suffering. Knowing that words can create happiness or suffering, I am determined to speak truthfully, with words that inspire self-confidence, joy, and hope. I will not spread news that I do not know to be certain and will not criticize or condemn things of which I am not sure. I will refrain from uttering words that can cause division or discord, or that can cause the family or the community to break. I am determined to make all efforts to reconcile and resolve all conflicts, however small.

(silence)

This is the fourth of the Five Mindfulness Trainings. Have you made an effort to study and practice it during the past two weeks?

(bell)

THE FIFTH OF THE FIVE MINDFULNESS TRAININGS

Aware of the suffering caused by unmindful consumption, I am committed to cultivating good health, both physical and mental, for myself, my family, and my society by practicing mindful eating, drinking, and consuming. I will ingest only items that preserve peace, well-being, and joy in my body, in my consciousness, and in the collective body and consciousness of my family and society. I am determined not to use alcohol or any other intoxicant or to ingest foods or other items that contain toxins, such as certain TV programs, magazines, books, films, and conversations. I am aware that to damage my body or my consciousness with these poisons is to betray my ancestors, my parents, my society, and future generations. I will work to transform violence, fear, anger, and confusion in myself and in society by practicing a diet for myself and for society. I understand that a proper diet is crucial for self-transformation and for the transformation of society.

(silence)

This is the fifth of the Five Mindfulness Trainings. Have you made an effort to study and practice it during the past two weeks?

(bell)

CONCLUDING WORDS

Brothers and Sisters, we have recited the Five Mindfulness Trainings, the foundation of happiness for the individual, the family, and society. We should recite them regularly so that our study and practice of the mindfulness trainings can deepen day by day.

Please join your palms and recite each line of the closing chant after me:

Reciting the trainings,
practicing the way of awareness,
gives rise to benefits without limit.
We vow to share the fruits with all beings.
We vow to offer tribute to parents, teachers, friends, and numerous beings
who give guidance and support along the path.

Contributors

Contributors

ROBERT AITKEN, ROSHI, is retired Head Teacher of the Diamond Sangha in Hawaii and cofounder of the Buddhist Peace Fellowship. He is author of *Encouraging Words, The Dragon Who Never Sleeps, The Mind of Clover, Taking the Path of Zen,* and *A Zen Wave.*

RICHARD BAKER, ROSHI, is Head Teacher of Crestone Mountain Zen Center in Colorado and of Dharma Sangha, Europe. He is the author of *Original Mind, the Practice of Zen in the West,* and cofounder of San Francisco, Tassajara, and Green Gulch Zen Centers.

STEPHEN BATCHELOR, Buddhist writer, translator, and teacher residing in England, is author of *The Awakening of the West: Buddhism and European Culture, The Faith to Doubt: Glimpses of Buddhist Uncertainty, Alone With Others: An Existential Approach to Buddhism, The Tibet Guide,* and translator of several texts from Tibetan.

PATRICIA MARX ELLSBERG is a social activist, public speaker, and workshop facilitator. Her life's work has been to bridge the political and spiritual worlds. Experienced in both Western politics and Eastern mystical traditions, she builds an unusual bond between essence and action.

JOAN HALIFAX, teacher, medical anthropologist, and founder of the Upaya Foundation, is author of *The Fruitful Darkness: Reconnecting with the Body of the Earth*, and coauthor of *The Human Encounter with Death*. She is a Dharma teacher in the Order of Interbeing.

CHÂN KHÔNG, a Buddhist nun, social worker, and assistant to Thich Nhat Hanh for over twenty years, is Director of Plum Village in France. She is author of *Learning True Love: How I Learned and Practiced Social Change in Vietnam*, and she is a Dharma teacher in the Order of Interbeing.

MAXINE HONG KINGSTON, winner of the National Book Award, is author of *The Woman Warrior: Memoirs of a Girlhood among Ghosts*, *China Men*, *Hawai'i One Summer*, and *Tripmaster Monkey: His Fake Book*. She is currently writing a *Book of Peace* on the transforming powers of warriors.

JACK KORNFIELD, Dharma teacher and cofounder of Spirit Rock Meditation Center in northern California, is author of *A Path with Heart: A Guide through the Perils and Promises of Spiritual Life* and *Living Buddhist Masters*, and coauthor of *Seeking the Heart of Wisdom: The Path of Insight Meditation*.

ANNABEL LAITY, a Buddhist nun and Dharma teacher in the Tiep Hien tradition, lives at Plum Village in France, where she helps lead the daily practice of mindfulness. She also leads retreats internationally, and is translator of many books by Thich Nhat Hanh.

CHRISTOPHER REED, founder of Ordinary Dharma and Manzanita Village meditation centers in southern California, is a Dharma teacher in the Order of Interbeing and author of numerous articles.

SULAK SIVARAKSA, founder of the International Network of Engaged Buddhists, based in Bangkok, and many other organizations, is a nominee for the 1993 Nobel Peace Prize. He is author of *Seeds of Peace: A Buddhist Vision for Renewing Society* and many other books.

GARY SNYDER, Pulitzer Prize-winning poet, lives in northern California. He is founder of the Ring of Bone Zendo, and author of *No Nature, The Practice of the Wild, Axe Handles, Turtle Island, Earth House Hold,* and many other books.

DAVID STEINDL-RAST, Benedictine monk, lives at a Camaldolese hermitage in California. He is author of *Gratefulness, The Heart of Prayer: An Approach to Life in Fullness,* and *A Listening Heart,* and is a leading figure in the movements for monastic renewal and East-West dialogue.

ARTHUR WASKOW is author of *Godwrestling, Seasons of Our Joy,* and *Down to Earth Judaism: Food, Money, Sex, and the Rest of Life,* and coauthor of *Becoming Brothers.* He is Director of The Shalom Center, a network of North American Jews committed to protecting the Earth from environmental disaster, and editor of *New Menorah,* a journal of Jewish renewal.

About the Author

Thich Nhat Hanh is a Buddhist monk, scholar, and poet. He served as Chair of the Vietnamese Buddhist Peace Delegation to the Paris Peace Talks and was nominated by Martin Luther King, Jr. for the Nobel Peace Prize. Author of many books, including *Living Buddha, Living Christ, Being Peace,* and *Peace Is Every Step,* he now lives in a small meditation community in France, where he writes, teaches, gardens, and helps refugees worldwide.

Parallax Press publishes books and tapes on mindful awareness and social responsibility, "making peace right in the moment we are alive." We carry all books and tapes of Thich Nhat Hanh. For a copy of our catalog, please write to:

Parallax Press
P.O. Box 7355
Berkeley, CA 94707
www.parallax.org